Remedy and Redemption

By

Anant Kumar Tripati LLM, Merit

Remedy and Redemption
A Legal Reference Guide

Copyright © 2018 By Anant Kumar Tripati

All rights Reserved. No part of this book may be reproduced or transmitted in any form by any means, graphic, electronic or mechanical including photocopying, recording, taping or by any information storage or retrieval system without written permission from publisher.

The purpose of this book is to inform, educate and entertain. Although every precaution has been taken in preparation of this book, there may be errors or omissions. Neither is any liability assumed for damages resulting, directly or indirectly, from the use of this information contained within this book.

Published by:
SureShot Books Publishing LLC
P.O. Box 924
Nyack, New York 10960
www.sureshotbooks.com

Libarary of Congress Cataloging-in-Publication Data

Remedy and Redemption.

This book has been published and made available as an e-book.

FOREWORD

This book has been painstakingly researched and written in hopes of enabling the basic humane treatment for all those incarcerated in the United States today and in the future.

THE AUTHOR

ANANT KUMAR TRIPATI LLM, Merit (2014)
UNIVERSITY OF LONDON
UNIVERSITY COLLEGE LONDON
QUEEN MARY UNIVERSITY OF LONDON

Mr. Tripati has specializations in Public International Law (2014), Public Law (2014), and European Law (2013).

NOTICE

This book is provided as a reference guide. Neither the publisher nor the author is offering or providing professional advice or services to the individual reader. The contents of this book are not intended to act as a substitute to consulting an attorney.

Neither the author nor publisher shall be liable or responsible for any loss or damage arising from any information or suggestion in this book.

"The Degree of a civilization can be judged by entering its prisons"
- Dostoyevsky. House of the Dead, 1862

TABLE OF CONTENTS

FOREWORD 1

INTRODUCTION 1

As stated in Living Designs Inc., et al., v   E.I.DuPont De Nemours And Company, et. Al., 431 F.3d 353 (9th Cir. 2005) 1

SETTING ASIDE JUDGMENTS FOR FRAUD UPON THE COURT 1

STATUTES OF LIMITATIONS 1

WHAT MUST THE COMPLAINT ALLEGE 1

JURISDICTION 1

THE PARTIES 2

SAMPLE COMPLAINT AGAINST ARIZONA ATTORNEY GENERAL AND DEPARTMENT OF CORRECTIONS 2

THE POLICY AT ISSUE 8

ROUTINE FAILURE TO FOLLOW RULES OF THE COURT IN DISCOVERY AND LITIGATION 8

IMPACT OF THEIR ACTION 9

RELIEF REQUESTED 9

SAMPLE COMPLAINT AGAINST WEXFORD HEALTH SOURCES 9

PARTIES 9

THE COMPLAINT 9

THE POLICY AT ISSUE 16

ROUTINE FAILURE TO FOLLOW RULES OF THE COURT IN DISCOVERY AND LITIGATION 16

IMPACT OF THEIR ACTION 16

RELIEF REQUESTED 16

RACKETEERING ACTION 16

STATUTES OF LIMITATIONS 17

JURISDICION AND VENUE 17

PARTIES 17

ENTERPRISE 17

CONTINUOUS PLUS 17

RICO CONSPIRACY 17

This would allow Corizon/Wexford nurses, grievance staff, providers, attorneys to be named as defendants 18

GOVERNMENT PROCESSES 18

INJURY 18

IMMUNE LITIGATION CONDUCT 18

PATTERN OF RACKETEERING ACTIVITY 18

SAMPLE COMPLAINT AGAINST CORIZON 18

PARTIES 18

1.   John Kristoffer Larsgard, Plaintiff, vs. Corizon Health, Inc., and DOES ONE TO TEN   Defendants.Defendants and each of them are persons capable of holding a legal or beneficial interest in property"   18 U.S.C. 1961(3) 18

BACKGROUND	18
JURISDICTION AND VENUE	19
ENTERPRISE	19
7. *Defendant authorized, requested, commanded, ratified, recklessly tolerated the unlawful conduct. It did so as a director, high management agent, acquiring or maintaining an interest in the business and profits of the enterprise , in furtherance of the business and activities of the enterprise.*	19
8. *Defendant conspired with members of the enterprise to violate 18 U.S.C. 1962(a)(b)(c)*	19
Defendant violated 18 U.S.C. 1962(a)(b)(c)(d).	19
CONTINUOUS PLUS	19
PATTERN OF RACKETEERING ACTIVITY	19
11. *Defendant violated 18 U.S.C. 1962(a)(b)(c)(d).*	29
INJURY	29
SAMPLE RACKETEERING COMPLAINT AGAINST WEXFORD HEALTH SOURCES	30
PARTIES	30
BACKGROUND	30
JURISDICTION AND VENUE	30
ENTERPRISE	30
7. *Defendant authorized, requested, commanded, ratified, recklessly tolerated the unlawful conduct. It did so as a director, high management agent, acquiring or maintaining an interest in the business and profits of the enterprise , in furtherance of the business and activities of the enterprise.*	30
8. *Defendant conspired with members of the enterprise to violate 18 U.S.C. 1962(a)(b)(c)*	30
CONTINUOUS PLUS	30
PATTERN OF RACKETEERING ACTIVITY	31
11. *Defendant violated 18 U.S.C. 1962(a)(b)(c)(d).*	37
INJURY	37
APPENDIX A	38
Barry Northcross Patterson, Plaintiff, vs. Charles L. Ryan, et al., Defendants.	38
APPENDIX B	51
STANLEY N. OZOROSKI, Appellant v. DR. FREDERICK R. MAUE, Chief of Clinical Services, Individually and in his official capacity; WEXFORD HEALTH SOURCES, INC.; PRISON HEALTH SERVICES, Individually and in its official capacity; DR. ADAM A. EDELMAN, Individually and in his official capacity; MARVA CERULLO, Health Care Administrator SCI Mahanoy, individually; CECILIA VALASQUEZ, Director of Guadenzia DRC; GAUDENZIA-DRC, All Defendants Jointly and Severally Liable; CHERYL CANTEY, Head Medical Supervisor of Gaudenzia DRC	51
APPENDIX C	55
John Kristoffer Larsgard, Plaintiff, vs. Corizon Health, Inc., Defendant.	55
APPENDIX D	65
CHARLES ISELEY, Appellant v. JEFFREY BEARD; ROBERT BITNER; KENNETH KYLER; FRANK GILLIS; WILMA SEWELL; KANDIS DASCANI; JOSEPH KORT, DIANA BANEY; PATRICIA EVERHART; PATRICIA YARGER; DAWN MILLS, Physician Asst.; PAUL ROEMER; MARY SHOWALTER; KILE; CYNTHIA STEVENS; JOHN SIDLER; PHS, INC.; ASG, INC.; WEXFORD HEALTH SERVICES, INC.	65
TABLE OF AUTHORITIES	69

INTRODUCTION

As stated in **Living Designs Inc., et al., v   E.I.DuPont De Nemours And Company, et. Al., 431 F.3d 353 (9th Cir. 2005)**

> "Membership in the bar is a privilege burdened with conditions. An attorney is received into that ancient fellowship for something more than private gain. He becomes an officer of the court and like the court itself,   an instrument or agency to advance the ends of justice."

In re Integration Of Nebraska State Bar Assn 275 N.W. 265, 268 (1937) provides

> An attorney owes his first duty to the court. He assumed his obligations toward it before he ever had a client. His oath requires him to be absolutely honest even though his client's interest may seem to require a contrary course. The (lawyer)cannot serve two masters and the one   (the lawyer has) undertaken to serve primarily is the court."

Very often lawyers who conceal/falsify evidence in their zeal to win forget their duties. As Living Designs states relying on DiSabatino v US Fidelity & Guaranty Co, 635 F.Supp. 35, 355 (D.De. 1986) when settlement is procured by fraud, it need not be shown there was a good cause of action at the time of the fraud. "The probable amount of settlement in the absence of fraud after considering all known or foreseeable facts and circumstances affecting the value of the claims on the date of settlement" is the issue. "Whether the defrauded part could have won its case is irrelevant to this calculation."

This book addresses just that showing avenues for seeking relief. Lawyers should refrain from fraudulent acts.

SETTING ASIDE JUDGMENTS FOR FRAUD UPON THE COURT

When the lawyer for the adverse party designs an unconscionable plan or scheme to improperly influence the court in its decision England v Doyle,   281 F.2d 304, 309-310 (9th cir. 1960) that judgment may be set aside for fraud upon the court. The United States Supreme Court has stated for at least ninety years that only "in the absence of fraud or collusion" does a judgment from a court with jurisdiction operate as res judicata.   Riehle v. Margolies, 279 U.S. 218, 225 (1929).

STATUTES OF LIMITATIONS

"There is no time limit on setting aside a judgment on "the ground of fraud upon the court nor can laches bar consideration of the matter. It does not matter whether a party bringing the fraud to the court's attention has clean hands." Wright Miler & Kane, Fed.   Prac. & Proc. Civil 2d. at 870, Page 412.

WHAT MUST THE COMPLAINT ALLEGE

JURISDICTION

As this is a federal question Title 28 U.S.C. 1331(1) provides federal courts with jurisdiction to entertain the complaint.

REMEDY AND REDEMPTION

THE PARTIES

The parties to the original complaint must be named as parties in the complaint alleging fraud upon the court. In the event the lawyers have also acted as policy makers and are the persons who form the custom and tradition of perpetrating fraud upon the court to prevail in litigation, then, as policy makers, they may be named as parties. Jeffes v Barnes, 208 F.3d 49, 57 (2nd Cir. 2000) Chew v Gates, 27 F.3d 1432, 1445 (9th Cir. 1994).

SAMPLE COMPLAINT AGAINST ARIZONA ATTORNEY GENERAL AND DEPARTMENT OF CORRECTIONS

1. In Barry Northcross Patterson, Plaintiff, vs. Charles L. Ryan, et al., Defendants. No. CV 05-1159-PHX-RCB (SPL) UNITED STATES DISTRICT COURT FOR THE DISTRICT OF ARIZONA A copy of the relevant decision is marked as Appendix A Plaintiff sued various employees of the Arizona Department Of Corrections for denial of his Kosher diet and retaliation. In accordance with the Paul Carter's unconscionable scheme to influence the court in it's decisions he concealed the following: (a) There are e.mails and internal documents in the form of memos, handwritten notes, inmate grievances which show that Linderman and other defendants have specifically put in place the practice to ensure that inmates who desire religious diets are not given these diets. These documents show that defendants are not entitled to qualified immunity because they denied plaintiff the diet, aware that they were violating the religious tenets of Plaintiff; (b)Carter also concealed e.mails, grievances, internal reports which show that other inmates have made similar complaints and Linderman with the approval of the director of the ARIZONA DEPARTMENT OF CORRECTIONS has put in place a practice to prevent inmates from practicing their religious tenets.(c) carter also concealed e.mails, grievances, appeals, internal documents showing that inmates who initiate litigation are retaliated against as a matter of routine practice; (d) carter also concealed communications between the office of the Arizona Attorney General and ADOC which are not-privileged. These communications show that employees of the Arizona Attorney General have approved the custom and practice to (i) prevent inmates from practicing their religious practices (ii) retaliating against those who litigate these issues (iii) concealing evidence to prevail in litigation.

2. It should be noted that the following are a few examples of cases in which the office of the Arizona Attorney General has engaged in fraud upon the court. These cases show the existence of a policy, custom, tradition.

    A. VICTOR ANTONIO PARSONS; SHAWN JENSEN; STEVE SWARTZ; DUSTIN BRISLAN; SONIA RODRIGUEZ; CHRISTINA VERDUZCO; JACKIE THOMAS; JEREMY SMITH; ROBERT CARRASCO GAMEZ, JR.; MARYANNE CHISHOLM; DESIREE LICCI; JOSEPH HEFNER; JOSHUA POLSON; CHARLOTTE WELLS; ARIZONA CENTER FOR DISABILITY LAW, Plaintiffs-Appellees, v. CHARLES L. RYAN; RICHARD PRATT, Defendants-Appellants. No. 13-16396 UNITED STATES COURT OF APPEALS FOR THE NINTH CIRCUIT

Through counsel Nicholas D. Acedo (argued) and Daniel P. Struck, Struck Wieneke & Love, P.L.C., Chandler, Arizona; Thomas C. Horne, Arizona Attorney General, and Michael E. Gottfried, Assistant Attorney General, Phoenix, Arizona, for Defendants-Appellants. Defendants concealed evidence that ADC's policies and practices governing medical care, dental care, and mental health care expose all inmates "to a substantial risk of serious harm, including unnecessary pain and suffering, preventable injury, amputation, disfigurement, and death." The plaintiffs support these general allegations with detailed references to nearly a dozen specific ADC policies and practices, including inadequate staffing, outright denials of care, lack of emergency treatment, failure to stock and provide critical medication, grossly substandard dental care, and failure to provide therapy and psychiatric medication to mentally ill inmates. They have employees and experts on staff who falsified discovery responses and documents to sustain their positions.

B. Robert F. Lindley, Jr., Plaintiff, vs. Charles L. Ryan, et al., Defendants. No. CV 12-1422-PHX-DGC (MEA) UNITED STATES DISTRICT COURT FOR THE DISTRICT OF ARIZONA

Through counsel For Charles L Ryan, Director AZ Dept of Corrections, John Kinton, named as acting Facility Health Administrator, Bruce J McMorran, named as Bruce McMorran Acting Facility Health Administrator, Unknown Truog, named as CO IV Correctional Officer, Defendants: Katherine Emiko Watanabe, LEAD ATTORNEY, Office of the Attorney General - Phoenix, Phoenix, AZ; Michael Evan Gottfried, LEAD ATTORNEY, Office of the Attorney General, Phoenix, AZ. They have employees and experts on staff who falsified discovery responses and documents to sustain their positions. Counsel concealed evidence that too many inmates have been denied care for cysts and other cancers causing them to die

C Eric SANCHEZ, Plaintiff-Appellant,v.Duane R. VILD, et al., Defendants-Appellees.No. 88-2458.United States Court of Appeals, Ninth Circuit. Through counsel Pamela J. Eaton, Asst. Atty. Gen., Phoenix, Ariz., for defendants-appellees.

They have employees and experts on staff who falsified discovery responses and documents to sustain their positions. Counsel concealed evidence that too many inmates have been denied care for similar medical conditions with permanent injury and death.

D. Anthony Merrick, Plaintiff, vs. Charles L. Ryan, et al., Defendants.No. CV 13-2386-PHX-RCB (BSB) UNITED STATES DISTRICT COURT FOR THE DISTRICT OF ARIZONA

Through counsel For Charles L Ryan, named as: Charles Ryan, Lance Hetmer, Mike Linderman, R Webster, Senior Chaplain, Unknown Kidwell, Chaplain, Delbert Henderson, named as: Senior Chaplain Henderson, James Miser, named as: Chaplain Miser, Melinda Stephan, named as: M. Stephan, Unknown Zaborsky, Defendants: Katherine Emiko Watanabe, LEAD ATTORNEY, Office of the Attorney General - Phoenix, Phoenix, AZ. counsel They have employees and experts on staff who generate false internal reports to sustain their positions and falsified discovery responses and documents to sustain their positions. Counsel concealed evidence that too many inmates who are not of the Christian faith have been denied materials and transferred as retaliation with ADOC employees generating false documents to sustain their action.

E. Erik Scott Maloney, Plaintiff, vs. Charles L. Ryan, et al., Defendants.No. CV 13-00314-PHX-RCB(BSB) UNITED STATES DISTRICT COURT FOR THE DISTRICT OF ARIZONA

Through counsel For Charles L Ryan, Director at Arizona Department of Corrections, Mike Linderman, Administrator of Pastoral Activities at Arizona Department of Corrections, Defendants: Neil Singh, LEAD ATTORNEY, Office of the Attorney General - Phoenix, Phoenix, AZ. They concealed the fact that it is defendants practice to prevent non-Christians from practicing their faith . They have employees and experts on staff who generate false internal reports to sustain their positions and falsified discovery responses and documents to sustain their positions.

F. Stephen Frank Karban, Plaintiff, vs. Charles Ryan, et al., Defendants No. CV 10-0406-TUC-DCB UNITED STATES DISTRICT COURT FOR THE DISTRICT OF ARIZONA

Through counsel For Charles L Ryan, Interim Director at Arizona Department of Corrections, Sandra Walker, Warden, Tucson Complex at Arizona Department of Corrections, Tara Hoyt, CO IV Grievance Coordinator, Winchester Unit at Arizona Department of Corrections, Karen Klausner, General Counsel to Director at Arizona Department of Corrections, Elizabeth Oros, CO IV Tucson Complex at Arizona Department of Corrections, Angelo

REMEDY AND REDEMPTION

Barry, Mailroom Sergeant , Tucson Complex Mailroom at Arizona Department of Corrections, Unknown Williams, Mail Clerk I, Tucson Complex Mailroom at Arizona Department of Corrections, Unknown Dossett, Appeals Officer, Central Office at Arizona Department of Corrections, Unknown Harrison, Offender Operations at Arizona Department of Corrections, Aurora Aguilar, Appeals Officer at Central Office at Arizona Department of Corrections, Defendants: Paul Edward Carter, Office of the Attorney General, Tucson, AZ. They concealed the fact that it is defendants practice to interfere with incoming legal research material .

G. Thomas M. James, Plaintiff, vs. Charles L. Ryan, et al., Defendants. No. CV 10-0510-PHX-GMS (JFM) UNITED STATES DISTRICT COURT FOR THE DISTRICT OF ARIZONA

Through counsel For Charles L Ryan, Defendant: Joseph Dean Estes, LEAD ATTORNEY, Office of the Attorney General - Phoenix, Phoenix, AZ They concealed the fact that inmates have no available remedies under PLRA as grievance staff have been directed no to afford inmates relief.. They have employees and experts on staff who generate false internal reports to sustain their positions and falsified discovery responses and documents to sustain their positions.

H. William Mark Isbell, Plaintiff, vs. Charles Ryan, et al., Defendants. No. CV 11-0391-PHX-JAT (JFM) UNITED STATES DISTRICT COURT FOR THE DISTRICT OF ARIZONA

For Charles L Ryan, Acting Director for A.D.O.C. at A.D.O.C. - Central Office. State employee employed by A.D.O.C. and acting under color of State Law. Sued in his official and individual capacities., Alfred Ramos, Deputy Warden of Arizona Department of Corrections (herein after A.D.O.C.), Arizona State Prison Complex (ASPC)-Eyman -Browning Unit. State employee employed by A.D.O.C. and acting under color of State Law. Sued in his official and individual capacities., Jack Heet, Associate Deputy Warden of A.D.O.C., Arizona State Prison Complex (ASPC) - Eyman - Browning Unit. State employee employed by A.D.O.C. and acting under color of State Law. Sued in his official and individual capacities., Ernie Trujillo, Warden of A.D.O.C., Arizona State Prison Complex (ASPC) - Eyman. State employee employed by A.D.O.C. and acting under color of State Law. Sued in his official and individual capacities., D Henderson, Senior Chaplain for A.D.O.C., Arizona State Prison Complex (ASPC) - Eyman. State employee employed by A.D.O.C. and acting under color of State Law. Sued in his official and individual capacities., A Miser, Chaplain for A.D.O.C., Arizona State Prison Complex (ASPC) - Eyman - Browning Unit, State employee employed by A.D.O.C. and acting under color of State Law. Sued in his official and individual capacities., Defendants: Wanda Ellen-Marie Hofmann, Office of the Attorney General, Liability Management Section, Tucson, AZ. . They have employees and experts on staff who falsified discovery responses and documents to sustain their positions. Counsel concealed evidence that too many inmates who are not of the Christian faith have been denied religious diets and transferred as retaliation with ADOC employees generating false documents to sustain their action.

I. David A. Higdon, Plaintiff, vs. Charles L. Ryan, Defendant. No. CV 13-0475-PHX-DGC (JFM) UNITED STATES DISTRICT COURT FOR THE DISTRICT OF ARIZONA

Through counsel For Charles L Ryan, Director of ADOC, Defendant: Michael Evan Gottfried, LEAD ATTORNEY, Office of the Attorney General, Phoenix, AZ. They concealed the fact that inmates who inform to protect others are not protected and that false disciplinary reports are the prevailing practice with the disciplinary proceedings being a sham. They have employees and experts on staff who generate false internal reports to sustain their positions and falsified discovery responses and documents to sustain their positions.

J. Karen Marie Hansen, Plaintiff, vs. Charles Ryan, et al., Defendants. No. CV 09-1290-PHX-GMS (ECV) UNITED STATES DISTRICT COURT FOR THE DISTRICT OF ARIZONA

Through counsel For Unknown Mitchell, Sgt./ ASPC - Mail and Property Sgt., Unknown Mims, Correctional Officer II/ ASPC - Mail and Property Officer, Ira Jones, CO III, Unknown Henderson-Rahman, named as Unknown

REMEDY AND REDEMPTION

Rahman - CO II, Michael Backes, named as Michael Backer - CO IV, Xavier Garcia, Tracy Thorton, Defendants: Paul Edward Carter, Office of the Attorney General, Liability Management Section, Tucson, AZ. They concealed the fact that they have employees and experts on staff who generate false internal reports to sustain their positions and falsified discovery responses and documents to sustain their positions.

K. AMMAR DEAN HALLOUM, Plaintiff, vs. CHARLES RYAN, et al., Defendants.No. CV 11-0097-PHX-RCB (JRI) UNITED STATES DISTRICT COURT FOR THE DISTRICT OF ARIZONA

Through counsel Kelley Joan Morrissey, Office of the Attorney General, Liability Management Section, Phoenix, AZ. Counsel concealed evidence that too many inmates who are not of the Christian faith have been denied practicing their with ADOC employees generating false documents to sustain their action. They have employees and experts on staff who falsified discovery responses and documents to sustain their positions.

L. Andre Almond Dennison, Plaintiff, v. Charles L. Ryan, et al., Defendants. No. CV-13-01925-PHX-SPL (ESW) UNITED STATES DISTRICT COURT FOR THE DISTRICT OF ARIZONA

Through counsel Charles L Ryan, named as Charles Ryan, Director of Prison Operations at AZ Dept of Corrections, Defendant: Katherine Emiko Watanabe, LEAD ATTORNEY, Office of the Attorney General - Phoenix, Phoenix, AZ. Kelley Joan Morrissey, Office of the Attorney General, Liability Management Section, Phoenix, AZ. Counsel concealed evidence that too many inmates have been denied practicing their with ADOC employees generating false documents to sustain their action. They have employees and experts on staff who falsified discovery responses and documents to sustain their positions.

M. David Arenberg, Plaintiff, vs. Charles Ryan, et al., Defendants.No. CV 10-2228-PHX-MHM (MHB)UNITED STATES DISTRICT COURT FOR THE DISTRICT OF ARIZONA

Through counsel For Charles L Ryan, named as Charles Ryan, Defendant: Alice Jolynn Rogers, Office of the Attorney General, Phoenix, AZ. Charles L Ryan, named as Charles Ryan, Director of Prison Operations at AZ Dept of Corrections, Defendant: Katherine Emiko Watanabe, LEAD ATTORNEY, Office of the Attorney General - Phoenix, Phoenix, AZ Counsel concealed evidence that too many inmates have been denied treatment for enlarged prostate, prescribed medication, and surgery if the medication did not work, very often dying. They have employees and experts on staff who falsified discovery responses and documents to sustain their positions.

N. Joseph Gerald Lee Eldridge, Plaintiff, vs. Charles L. Ryan, et al., Defendants.No. CV 13-0888-PHX-DGC (JFM)UNITED STATES DISTRICT COURT FOR THE DISTRICT OF ARIZONA

Through counsel For Charles L Ryan, named as: Charles Ryan - Director, Stacey Crabtree, Bureau Administrator, Unknown Willams, CO II, Defendants: Michael John Hrnicek, LEAD ATTORNEY, Office of the Attorney General - Phoenix - Liability Mgmt., Phoenix, AZ. Counsel concealed evidence that too many inmates have been denied placement in protective custody or in a sex-offender yard with knowledge they have been labeled a snitch, and that they have been assaulted by other inmates as a result. They have employees and experts on staff who falsified discovery responses and documents to sustain their positions and generate false internal reports to sustain their actions.

O. Jeffrey James Faulkner, Plaintiff, vs. Charles Ryan, Defendant.No. CV 10-2441-PHX-SMM (JFM) UNITED STATES DISTRICT COURT FOR THE DISTRICT OF ARIZONAThrough counsel For Charles L Ryan, named as Charles Ryan, Director of ADOC prisons, Defendant: Michael Evan Gottfried, Office of the Attorney General, Phoenix, AZ.

Counsel concealed evidence that too many inmates are confined indefinitely in punitive, isolated administrative detention pursuant to a policy enforced and upheld by Defendant and released only when they become a snitch, which threatens Plaintiff's safety. They have employees and experts on staff who falsified discovery responses and documents to sustain their positions and generate false internal reports to sustain their actions.

- P. Ace B. Freemon, Plaintiff, vs. Charles Ryan, et al., Defendants No. CV 09-1717-PHX-JAT (JRI) UNITED STATES DISTRICT COURT FOR THE DISTRICT OF ARIZONA

Through counsel For Charles L Ryan, in his Individual and Official Capacity as acting Director of the Arizona Department of Corrections, J Freeland, in his Individual and official capacity as Deputy Warden of the Arizona Department of Correction - Browning Unit prison, and as acting STG Committee member of the Arizona Department of Corrections, Robert Patton, in his Individual and offical capacity as acting STG Committee chair member of the Arizona Department of Correction, R Bock, in his Individual and official capacity as acting STG committee member of the Arizona Department of Corrections, J Kimble, in his Individual and official capacity as acting STG committee member of the Arizona Department of Corrections, George Smith, originally named as M Smith - Lt., in his Individual and Official capacity as acting STG coordinator of the Arizona Department of Corrections, Lisa Celaya, in her Individual and Official Capacity As acting STG investigator, central office of the Department of Corrections, Defendants: Michael Evan Gottfried, Office of the Attorney General, Phoenix, AZ. Counsel concealed evidence that too many inmates are confined indefinitely in punitive, isolated administrative detention pursuant to a policy enforced and upheld by Defendant and released only when they become a snitch, which threatens Plaintiff's safety. They fail to provide sufficient notice of the allegations and thereby denied inmates the opportunity to question witnesses. Defendants have the practice to deny inmates a fair opportunity to question witnesses. They have employees and experts on staff who falsified discovery responses and documents to sustain their positions and generate false internal reports to sustain their actions.

- Q. Mark E. Hampton, Plaintiff, vs. Charles Ryan, et al., Defendants.No. CV 03-1706-PHX-NVWUNITED STATES DISTRICT COURT FOR THE DISTRICT OF ARIZONA

Through counsel For Charles Ryan, Dora B Schriro, Dora Schriro, Conrad Luna, sued in his individual & official capacity, Barbara Shearer, sued in her individual & official capacity, Defendants: Catherine Marie Bohland, Office of the Attorney General, Phoenix, AZ. . Through counsel For Charles L Ryan, named as Charles Ryan, Director of ADOC prisons, Defendant: Michael Evan Gottfried, Office of the Attorney General, Phoenix, AZ. Counsel concealed evidence that too many inmates are confined indefinitely in punitive, isolated administrative detention pursuant to a policy enforced and upheld by Defendant and released only when they become a snitch, which threatens Plaintiff's safety. They have employees and experts on staff who falsified discovery responses and documents to sustain their positions and generate false internal reports to sustain their actions.

- R. Chad Lucas Harrison, Plaintiff, v. Charles L. Ryan, et al., Defendants. No. CV-13-01152-PHX-DLR (ESW)UNITED STATES DISTRICT COURT FOR THE DISTRICT OF ARIZONA

Through counsel For Charles L Ryan, Director of State Prisons, Stacey Crabtree, OSB Administrator at Central Office, Defendants: Katherine Emiko Watanabe, LEAD ATTORNEY, Office of the Attorney General - Phoenix, Phoenix, AZ. Counsel concealed e-mails, grievances, inmate letters and complaints, classification documents and appeals documents relating to total number of assaults physical and sexual assaults. They have employees and experts on staff who falsified discovery responses and documents to sustain their positions and generate false internal reports to sustain their actions.

- S. Shaka, Plaintiff, v. Charles Ryan, et al., Defendants.No. CV 10-2253-PHX-SMM (BSB) UNITED STATES DISTRICT COURT FOR THE DISTRICT OF ARIZONA

Through counsel For Charles L Ryan, named as Chuck Ryan, Director, AZ Department of Corrections at Central Office, Phoenix, AZ, Dennis G Chenail, named as Dennis Chenail; Facility Health Administrator at Yuma Complex,

REMEDY AND REDEMPTION

San Luis, AZ, Defendants: Paul Edward Carter, Office of the Attorney General, Liability Management Section, Tucson, AZ. Counsel concealed evidence that Inmates are often not seen by specialists until it is too late, They have employees and experts on staff who falsified discovery responses and documents to sustain their positions and generate false internal reports to sustain their actions

T.FRANCISCO ROBINSON, Plaintiff/Appellant, v. CHARLES RYAN, as Director, Arizona Department of Corrections; Regina Dorsey; Anna Gonzales; David Summers; Karyn Klausner, Defendants/Appellees. No. 1 CA- CV 12-0535COURT OF APPEALS OF ARIZONA, DIVISION ONE

Arizona Attorney General's Office, Phoenix, By Michael E. Gottfried, Counsel for Defendants/Appellees. Concealed evidence that there are too many instances when other inmates plant contraband on inmates but the prison authorities do not conduct thorough and meaningful investigation of the facts. , They have employees and experts on staff who falsified discovery responses and documents to sustain their positions and generate false internal reports to sustain their actions

U. JOHN P. BAKER, Plaintiff/Appellant, v. D. CARRILLO and CHARLES RYAN, Defendants/Appellees.2 CA-CV 2011-0048COURT OF APPEALS OF ARIZONA, DIVISION TWO, DEPARTMENT A

Thomas C. Horne, Arizona Attorney General, By Paul E. Carter, Tucson, Attorneys for Defendants/Appellees. concealed evidence that there are too many instances when ADOC employees allow inmates with gang affiliation to be housed with "regular" inmates "subjecting inmates to gang verbal threats and other disruptive behavior.

V. AMIN RAHMAN SHAKUR, Plaintiff/Appellant, v. DORA B. SCHRIRO; CHARLES RYAN, Defendants/Appellees.No. 1 CA-CV 10-0530COURT OF APPEALS OF ARIZONA, DIVISION ONE, DEPARTMENT E

For Defendants/Appellees: Kelley J. Morrissey, Assistant Attorney General, Thomas C. Horne, Arizona Attorney General, Phoenix. . concealed evidence that there are too many instances when ADOC has breached settlement agreements and retaliates against those who prevail.

W. JOHN P. BAKER, Plaintiff/Appellant, v. TERRY L. STEWART, CHARLES RYAN, STEVEN LYNCH, DARYL JOHNSON, THOMAS LUTZ, GARY PINKSTAFF, GARY L. ULLOM, DANIEL R. GARVIN, CO4 TUCKER, LORRAINE ROLNICK, CO3 KNOLL, SCOTT SCHMIER, BETTY ULIBARRI, KATHY COOPER, PATRICIA STAPLER, FRANCES CAPPADOCIA, LPN GONZALES, and RICKEY LEWIS, Defendants/Appellees.2 CA-CV 2002-0109COURT OF APPEALS OF ARIZONA, DIVISION TWO, DEPARTMENT B

Terry Goddard, Arizona Attorney General, By Wanda E. Hofmann, Tucson, Attorneys for Defendants/Appellees. . concealed evidence that there are too many instances when ADOC has delayed/denied treatment for inmates, refusing to perform timely surgery. They have employees and experts on staff who falsified discovery responses and documents to sustain their positions and generate false internal reports to sustain their actions

X. Peter Sotelo, Plaintiff, vs. Terry Stewart; Donna Clement; Charles Ryan; Meg Savage; Dora Shriro, et. al., Defendants.No. CV 03-1668-PHX-NVW UNITED STATES DISTRICT COURT FOR THE DISTRICT OF ARIZONA

For Terry Stewart, sued in his official capacity, Charles L Ryan, sued in his official capacity, Dora Schriro, sued in her official capacity, Meg Savage, sued in her official capacity, Dona H Clement, sued in her official capacity, Defendants: James Randall Jue, Office of the Attorney General, Liability Management Section, Phoenix, AZ. . concealed evidence that there are too many instances when ADOC has denied protective housing which causes sexual assaults, discrimination and death threats at the hands of other prisoners. Prison officials have repeatedly failed to take notice of and prosecute the perpetrators of offenses against such inmates. They have employees and experts on staff who falsified discovery responses and documents to sustain their positions and generate false internal reports to sustain their actions

    Y. David Standley, Plaintiff, v. Charles Ryan, et al., DefendantsNo. CV 10-1867-PHX-DGC (ECV)UNITED STATES DISTRICT COURT FOR THE DISTRICT OF ARIZONA

For Charles L Ryan, named as Charles Ryan; Director of ADOC, Alfred Ramos, Deputy Warden of ADOC, Browning Unit also known as A Ramos, Jeffrey Freeland, Acting STG Committee Chair Member for ADOC also known as J Freeland, H Matson, Deputy Warden at ADOC, J James, Deputy Warden at ADOC, Robert Patton, Acting STGVC Chair/Security Operations Officer Administrator for ADOC also known as R Patton, R Yesenski, Lt., Acting STG Coordinator for ADOC, Defendants: Michael Evan Gottfried, Office of the Attorney General, Phoenix, AZ. concealed evidence that while in theory STG policy is an effort to control prison gang activity in Arizona's prisons and minimize the threat posed by gangs there are too many instances when the policy has been used to target persons for no just cause and the review process is unable to take corrective actions for the reviewers have been so directed. They have employees and experts on staff who falsified discovery responses and documents to sustain their positions and generate false internal reports to sustain their actions

    AA. Thomas Stewart, Jr., Plaintiff, vs. Charles L. Ryan, et al., Defendants.No. CV 12-0719-PHX-RCB (LOA)UNITED STATES DISTRICT COURT FOR THE DISTRICT OF ARIZONA

For Karen Barcklay-Dodson, named as Dr. K. Barcklay-Dodson, "et al.", Defendant: Claudia Acosta Collings, LEAD ATTORNEY, Office of the Attorney General - Tucson, Tucson, AZ. concealed evidence that ADOC has a history of denying treatment for conditions such as spinal stenosis and disc degeneration and bulging They have employees and experts on staff who falsified discovery responses and documents to sustain their positions and generate false internal reports to sustain their actions

    BB. Sheldon Walker, Plaintiff, v. Charles L. Ryan, et al., Defendants.No. CV-14-02554-PHX-DJH ZB) UNITED STATES DISTRICT COURT FOR THE DISTRICT OF ARIZONA

For Charles L Ryan, Director of Arizona Department of Corrections at Central Office, Mike Linderman, Administrator of Pastoral Activities at Central Office, Unknown Vicklund, Senior Chaplain at Eyman Complex, Defendants: Kelley Joan Morrissey, LEAD ATTORNEY, Office of the Attorney General, Liability Management Section, Phoenix, AZ. Concealed evidence there are too many instances when non-Christian inmates are prevented from practicing their religion. They have employees and experts on staff who falsified discovery responses and documents to sustain their positions and generate false internal reports to sustain their actions

THE POLICY AT ISSUE

In the above example the allegation should be something like this:

> "Brnovich has implemented the custom and tradition in
> Which members of his firm perpetrate fraud upon the court
> to prevail in litigation. Specifically they conceal evidence,
> manufacture evidence and submit false declarations to improperly
> influence the courts in their decisions. This unconscionable plan
> has employees such as Carter and others set forth in this complaint,
> among others, perpetrate fraud upon the court."

**ROUTINE FAILURE TO FOLLOW RULES OF THE
COURT IN DISCOVERY AND LITIGATION**

REMEDY AND REDEMPTION

Redman v County Of San Diego, 942 F.2d 1435, 1445 (9th Cir. 1991)(en banc) states routine failure to follow written rules hold the defendants liable. Defendants, and each of them, as discussed above routinely fail to follow the provisions of Federal Rules Of Civil Procedure 26 through 37 pursuant to their unconscionable scheme to influence the courts.

IMPACT OF THEIR ACTION

As a direct consequence of their failure plaintiff did not prevail in the litigation. But for their actions plaintiff would have prevailed.

RELIEF REQUESTED

Plaintiff demands a trial by jury, damages and for an order declaring the judgment void due to fraud upon the court, costs, fees and such other relief as the court may deem fit and proper.

<u>SAMPLE COMPLAINT AGAINST WEXFORD HEALTH SOURCES</u>

<u>PARTIES</u>

STANLEY N. OZOROSKI, Appellant v. DR. FREDERICK R. MAUE, Chief of Clinical Services, Individually and in his official capacity; WEXFORD HEALTH SOURCES, INC.; PRISON HEALTH SERVICES, Individually and in its official capacity; DR. ADAM A. EDELMAN, Individually and in his official capacity; MARVA CERULLO, Health Care Administrator SCI Mahanoy, individually; CECILIA VALASQUEZ, Director of Guadenzia DRC; GAUDENZIA-DRC, All Defendants Jointly and Severally Liable; CHERYL CANTEY, Head Medical Supervisor of Gaudenzia Samuel H. Foreman, Esq., Leah M. Lewis, Esq., Weber, Gallagher, Simpson, Stapleton, Fires & Newby, Pittsburgh, PA.

<u>THE COMPLAINT</u>

1. Plaintiff suffered a small bowel perforation during a hernia repair operation in 1993. The surgery was delayed after repeated complaints. As a result, Ozoroski underwent multiple corrective surgeries shortly thereafter. Despite ongoing treatment, however, Ozoroski continued to experience abdominal problems and developed an enterocutaneous fistula. Wexford through Samuel H. Foreman, Esq., Leah M. Lewis, Esq., Weber, Gallagher, Simpson, Stapleton, Fires & Newby, Pittsburgh, PA. has devised an unconscionable plan to influence the court. Pursuant to this plan (a) Wexford conceals e.mails, records, reports concerning similar complaints; (b) it conceals the fact that it does not treat inmates and asks prison systems not to provide treatment that is expensive. (c) it also conceals evidence of the fact that it has on staff and retainer doctors and experts who have agreed for a fee to provide whatever testimony Wexford desires to defeat inmate complaints. Acting pursuant to this plan Wexford concealed this evidence A Copy Of The Decision is marked Appendix B. Wexford concealed the fact that it has the practice of delaying hernia surgery and that plaintiff would not have been disabled as its expert testified.

A. Set forth below are other examples of litigation fraud by counsel for Wexford pursuant to the unconscionable plan designed by Samuel H. Foreman, Esq., Leah M. Lewis, Esq., Weber, Gallagher, Simpson, Stapleton, Fires & Newby, Pittsburgh, PA.

B. Galen Lloyd Houser, Plaintiff -vs- Charles L. Ryan, et al., Defendants. CV-13-0200-PHX-GMS (JFM) UNITED STATES DISTRICT COURT FOR THE DISTRICT OF ARIZONA

Wexford has retained staff who issue whatever declaration/expert report is necessary to defeat claims. Through counsel who have first hand knowledge through information gained through prior litigation For Wexford Health Sources Incorporated, ADC Contracted Health Care, Provider for the State of Arizona,

REMEDY AND REDEMPTION

(outside the State of Arizona, location not known.), Defendant: Brandi Christine Blair, Edward G Hochuli, LEAD ATTORNEYS, Jones Skelton & Hochuli PLC, Phoenix, AZ. Concealed evidence that Defendant Wexford through the nation has had its contracts cancelled for violating various terms of its contract by failing to provide Plaintiff medical treatment, instituting policies requiring the termination "en masse" of the provision of various medications,

C. Robert Joseph Benge, Plaintiff, v. Charles L. Ryan, et al., Defendants.No. CV 14-0402-PHX-DGC (BSB)UNITED STATES DISTRICT COURT FOR THE DISTRICT OF ARIZONA.

Through counsel For Wexford Health Incorporated of Pittsburgh, PA, Defendant: Brandi Christine Blair, Edward G Hochuli, Kenneth Louis Moskow, LEAD ATTORNEYS, Jones Skelton & Hochuli PLC, Phoenix, AZ. Wexford concealed evidence that it is the norm for them to deny treatment for fractures until it is too late, discontinue prescription medications.

D. TOMMY WHITE, SR., Plaintiff-Appellant v. CHRISTOPHER B. EPPS, COMMISSIONER, MISSISSIPPI DEPARTMENT OF CORRECTIONS; RON KING, Superintendent, South Mississippi Correctional Institution-Two; DR. RON WOODALL; NURSE HAM; WEXFORD HEALTH; NURSE APRIL MEGS, Defendants-AppelleesNo. 10-60556 UNITED STATES COURT OF APPEALS FOR THE FIFTH CIRCUIT

Wexford has retained staff who issue whatever declaration/expert report is necessary to defeat claims. Through counsel who have first hand knowledge through information gained through prior litigation. For CHRISTOPHER B EPPS, COMMISSIONER, MISSISSIPPI DEPARTMENT OF CORRECTIONS, RON KING, Superintendent, South Mississippi Correctional Institution-Two, Defendants - Appellees: Charles Baron Irvin, Esq., Office of the Attorney General for the State of Mississippi, Jackson, MS. For RON WOODALL, Doctor, HAM, Nurse, WEXFORD HEALTH, APRIL MEGS, Nurse, Defendants - Appellees: Vardaman Kimball Smith, III, Bryan Nelson, P.A., Hattiesburg, MS. Concealed evidence that inmates have no remedy under PLRA for grievance staff have been directed not to afford relief.

E. TIMOTHY G PRYER, Plaintiff-Appellant v. R. WALKER, Doctor/Health Services Administrator at CMCF III; SHARON PAIGE, Captain, Central MS Correctional Facility III; DR. JOSEPH BLACKSTON; CORRECTIONAL HEALTH SERVICE, INC.; WEXFORD HEALTHCARE RESOURCES; COMMISSIONER CHRISOPHER EPPS; MARGARET BINGHAM, Defendants-AppelleesNo. 08-60867 UNITED STATES COURT OF APPEALS FOR THE FIFTH CIRCUIT

For R WALKER, Doctor/Health Services Administrator at CMCF III, CORRECTIONAL HEALTH SERVICE, Defendants - Appellees: Saundra Brown Strong, Phelps Dunbar, L.L.P., Jackson, MS.For SHARON PAIGE, Captain, Central MS Correctional Facility III, COMMISSIONER CHRISOPHER EPPS, MARGARET BINGHAM, Defendants - Appellees: Charles Baron Irvin, Esq., Pelicia E. Hall, Esq., Special Assistant Attorney General, Office of the Attorney General, for the State of Mississippi, Jackson, MS.For WEXFORD HEALTHCARE RESOURCES, Defendant - Appellee: Joseph A. O'Connell, III, Esq., Vardaman Kimball Smith, III, Bryan Nelson, P.A., Hattiesburg, MS. Wexford has retained staff who issue whatever declaration/expert report is necessary to defeat claims. Through counsel who have first hand knowledge through information gained through prior litigation Concealed evidence that IT IS THE NORM NOT TO PROPERLY DIAGNOSE AND TREAT INMATES CAUSING NUMEROUS DEATHS AND PERMANENT INJURY

F. JESSICA HANKEY, Individually, and as Administratrix of the Estate of Ryan Rohrbaugh, Appellant v. WEXFORD HEALTH SOURCES, INC.; PRISON HEALTH SERVICES, INC.; D.O. MARK BAKER; D.O. ALAN ESPER; DEBORAH O'LEARY, PA-C No. 09-3675 UNITED STATES COURT OF APPEALS FOR THE THIRD CIRCUIT

REMEDY AND REDEMPTION

For JESSICA HANKEY, Individually and as Administratix of the Estate of Ryan Rohrbaugh, Plaintiff - Appellant: Charles W. Marsar, Jr., Esq., Harrisburg, PA.For WEXFORD HEALTH SOURCES, INC., Defendant - Appellee: Patricia L. Dodge, Esq., Joshua R. Lorenz, Esq., Meyer, Unkovic & Scott, Pittsburgh, PA.For O'LEARY, Defendant - Non-Participating: Patricia L. Dodge, Esq., Joshua R. Lorenz, Esq., Meyer, Unkovic & Scott, Pittsburgh, PA.For MARK BAKER, Doctor, Defendant - Appellee: William D. Kennedy, Esq., Rosemary R. Schnall, Esq., White & Williams, Berwyn, PA. Through counsel Wexford concealed they give significant treatment but delay/deny being examined by specialists and that as a direct result the treatment is not effective, causing permanent injury and deaths. Wexford has retained staff who issue whatever declaration/expert report is necessary to defeat claims.

G. KENNETH F. LEONARD, Plaintiff/Appellant, v. FLORIDA DEPARTMENT OF CORRECTIONS, WEXFORD HEALTH SOURCES, INC., DAVID HARRIS, G. SOMODEVILLA, A. PIPIN, J.L. GREEN, AND G.J. SMITH, Defendants/Appellees. 06-11223-FF UNITED STATES COURT OF APPEALS FOR THE ELEVENTH CIRCUIT

Through counsel RITTER CHUSID BIVONA & COHEN, LLP, MITCHEL CHUSID, ESQ., Florida Bar No. 879282, Attorneys for Wexford Health Sources, Inc., Guillermo Somodevilla, and Gail Smith Wexford concealed the fact there are too many instances where it has failed to give medically prescribed supplies causing inmates to suffer. Wexford has retained staff who issue whatever declaration/expert report is necessary to defeat claims.

H. CONTRELL PLUMMER, Plaintiff-Appellant, v. WEXFORD HEALTH SOURCES, INCORPORATED, et al., Defendants-Appellees.No. 14-3314UNITED STATES COURT OF APPEALS FOR THE SEVENTH CIRCUIT

For Wexford Health Sources, Incorporated, MAGID FAHIM, Doctor, Medical Director of Menard, FE FUENTES, Doctor, Defendants - Appellees: Timothy Patrick Dugan, Attorney, Sandberg Phoenix & Von Gontard P.C., St. Louis, MO. Concealed evidence they follow the ineffective course of treatment causing permanent injury and death. Wexford has retained staff who issue whatever declaration/expert report is necessary to defeat claims.

I. RONALD C. MACON, JR., Plaintiff-Appellant, v. SYLVIA MAHONE, DENNIS LARSON, and WEXFORD HEALTH SOURCES, INC., Defendants-Appellees. No. 13-2155 UNITED STATES COURT OF APPEALS FOR THE SEVENTH CIRCUIT

For Sylvia Mahone, Dennis Larson, Wexford Health Sources, Incorporated, Defendants - Appellees (13-2155): Michael John Charysh, Attorney, Charysh & Schroeder, Ltd., Chicago, IL CONCEALED EVIDENCE IINMATES ARE DYING AND PERMANENT INJURY IS CAYSED OFTEN BY THEIR PRACTICE OF DELAYING/DENYING TREATMENT FOR failing kidneys Wexford has retained staff who issue whatever declaration/expert report is necessary to defeat claims.

J. JUSTIN JAMES HINZO, Plaintiff - Appellant, v. NEW MEXICO CORRECTIONS DEPARTMENT; JOE WILLIAMS; GEORGE TAPIA; WEXFORD HEALTH SOURCES, INC.; CORRECTIONAL MEDICAL SERVICES, INC.; DR. FNU ARNOLD; DR. WILLIAM MIZELL; DR. TONY LNU; DR. DEBRA CLYDE; DR. JOHN STOVER; DR. JOHN DOE (L.C.C.F.); DR. JOHN DOE (C.N.M.C.F.); DR. JOHN DOE (W.N.M.C.F.); DAVID GONZALES, Correctional Officer; WAYNE GALLEGOS; LIANE LOPEZ, R.N.; JERRY ROARK (Deputy Warden); LAWRENCE JARAMILLO, Warden P.N.M.; G.E.O., Defendants - Appellees. No 13-2060UNITED STATES COURT OF APPEALS FOR THE TENTH CIRCUIT

Counsel For WEXFORD MEDICAL SERVICES, Defendant - Appellee: Sebastian A. Dunlap, Edward W. Shepherd, Allen, Shepherd, Lewis & Syra, Albuquerque, NM. For DAVID GONZALES, Defendant - Appel-

REMEDY AND REDEMPTION

lee: Melinda L. Wolinsky, New Mexico Corrections Department, Office of General Counsel, Santa Fe, NM. CONCEALED evidence they deny/delay treatment and has retained staff who issue whatever declaration/expert report is necessary to defeat claims often false.

K. MANNIE MADDOX, Plaintiff--Appellant, v. WEXFORD HEALTH SOURCES, INC., et al., Defendnts--Appellees.No. 12-1810UNITED STATES COURT OF APPEALS FOR THE SEVENTH CIRCUIT

For WEXFORD HEALTH SOURCES, INCORPORATED, Defendant - Appellee: Brad A. Elward, Attorney, HEYL, ROYSTER, VOELKER & ALLEN, Peoria, IL.For PETER H. KEHOE, Defendant - Appellee: Jack Kiley, Attorney, ERICKSON, DAVIS, MURPHY, JOHNSON, GRIFFITH & WALSH, Decatur, IL.For MARY MILLER, Defendant - Appellee: Carl J. Elitz, Attorney, OFFICE OF THE ATTORNEY GENERAL, Civil Appeals Division, Chicago, IL. Concealed evidence it is the norm to deny/delay treatment for impaired causing loss very often of the vision. Wexford has retained staff who issue whatever declaration/expert report is necessary to defeat claims.

L. JAMES MATHEW HARRIS, Plaintiff-Appellant, versus CHRISTOPHER B. EPPS, Commissioner, Mississippi Department of Corrections; GLORIA PERRY, Doctor; ROBERT MOORE, Doctor; DAISY THOMAS, Doctor; RONALD WOODALL, Doctor; KEN KAISER, Doctor; JOHN DOE; WEXFORD HEALTH SOURCES, INCORPORATED, Also Known as Wexford Health Services, Defendants-Appellees.No. 12-60701 UNITED STATES COURT OF APPEALS FOR THE FIFTH CIRCUIT

For ROBERT MOORE, Doctor, DAISY THOMAS, Doctor, RONALD WOODALL, Doctor, KEN KAISER, Doctor, WEXFORD HEALTH SOURCES, INCORPORATED, also known as Wexford Health Services, Defendants - Appellees: Vardaman Kimball Smith, III, Bryan Nelson, P.A., Hattiesburg, MS. Concealed evidence they as a matter of practice deny treatment for Hepatitis C infection and back problems. Wexford has retained staff who issue whatever declaration/expert report is necessary to defeat claims.

M. DORCUS WITHERS, Plaintiff-Appellant, v. WEXFORD HEALTH SOURCES, INC., et al., Defendants-Appellees.No. 10-3012 UNITED STATES COURT OF APPEALS FOR THE SEVENTH CIRCUIT

For LOIS MATHES, GERARDO ACEVEDO, Defendants - Appellees: Rachel A. Murphy, Attorney, OFFICE OF THE ATTORNEY GENERAL, Civil Appeals Division, Chicago, IL. For WEXFORD HEALTH SOURCES, INCORPORATED, DEBRA MILLER, R.N., Defendants - Appellees: Brad A. Elward, Attorney, Craig L. Unrath, Attorney, HEYL, ROYSTER, VOELKER & ALLEN, Peoria, IL. Concealed evidence it denies effective treatment for scoliosis, which is lateral curvature of the spine; on an x-ray the spine appears from the front or back to be S- or C-shaped rather than I-shaped. Wexford has retained staff who issue whatever declaration/expert report is necessary to defeat claims.

N. HOYT RAY, Plaintiff-Appellant, v. WEXFORD HEALTH SOURCES, INC., and VIPIN K. SHAH, Defendants-Appellees.No. 12-1774 UNITED STATES COURT OF APPEALS FOR THE SEVENTH CIRCUIT

For WEXFORD HEALTH SOURCES, INCORPORATED, VIPIN K. SHAH, Doctor, Defendants - Appellees: Tamara K. Hackmann, Attorney, HEYL, ROYSTER, VOELKER & ALLEN, Urbana, IL; Matthew Lurkins, Attorney, HEYL, ROYSTER, VOELKER & ALLEN, Springfield, IL; Craig L. Unrath, Attorney, HEYL, ROYSTER, VOELKER & ALLEN, Peoria, IL. . Concealed evidence it denies effective treatment for pain. It examines the patient but does not follow community standards to ensure treatment is effective. Wexford has retained staff who issue whatever declaration/expert report is necessary to defeat claims.

O. WILLIAM L. LANE, Plaintiff-Appellant, v. WEXFORD HEALTH SOURCES (CONTREATOR); VANESSA SAWYER, Health Care Administrator; PAMILA REDDEN, Defendants-Appellees.No. 11-3552 UNITED STATES COURT OF APPEALS FOR THE SIXTH CIRCUIT

For WEXFORD HEALTH SOURCES (CONTREATOR), PAMILA REDDEN, Defendants - Appellees: Paul-Michael La Fayette, Poling Petrello, Columbus, OH. . Concealed evidence it denies treatment for those disabled with gun shot wounds or discrepancy between the length of his legs. It examines the patient but does not follow community standards to ensure treatment is effective denying special needs to manage such conditions. Wexford has retained staff who issue whatever declaration/expert report is necessary to defeat claims.

P. SOTINA LAVALE CUFFEE, deceased, Estate of, by and through her administrator, Bradley A. Cuffee, Plaintiff - Appellant, v. JOHN R. NEWHART, individually and in his official capacity as Sheriff of the City of Chesapeake, Defendant - Appellee, v. WEXFORD HEALTH SOURCES, INCORPORATED, Third Party Defendant - Appellee.No. 10-1494UNITED STATES COURT OF APPEALS FOR THE FOURTH CIRCUIT

Andrew J. Terrell, Thomas C. Mugavero, WHITEFORD, TAYLOR & PRESTON, LLP, Falls Church, Virginia, for Appellee Wexford Health Sources, Incorporated. . Concealed evidence it denies/delays treatment for those with painful toothache, of severe chest pains, tingling in arms and back, and insomnia frequently causing death. It examines the patient but does not follow community standards to ensure treatment is effective denying special needs to manage such conditions. Wexford has retained staff who issue whatever declaration/expert report is necessary to defeat claims

Q. DAVON LYMON, Plaintiff-Appellant, v. ARAMARK CORPORATION; JOSEPH NEUBAUER; CHARLIE CARRIZALES, Defendants, and WEXFORD CORPORATION, JOHN SANCHEZ; ABNER HERNANDEZ; JOE WILLIAMS; NEW MEXICO DEPARTMENT OF CORRECTIONS, Defendants-Appellees. No. 11-2210 UNITED STATES COURT OF APPEALS FOR THE TENTH CIRCUIT

For WEXFORD CORPORATION, Defendant - Appellee: James Roy Wood, Miller Stratvert, Albuquerque, NM. . Concealed evidence it denies/delays treatment for those injured in prison often causing permanent injury.

R. PAUL GRAHAME MORGAN, Plaintiff-Appellant v. STATE OF MISSISSIPPI; ATTORNEY GENERAL OF THE STATE OF MISSISSIPPI; CHRISTOPHER EPPS; E.L. SPARKMAN; RONALD KING; LAWRENCE KELLY; MARGARET BINGHAM; BOBBY KING; DR. BEARRY; RUTHIE HALL, Nurse; MILLIS WASHINGTON; DR. ARNOLD; DR. WALKER; LT. HOLMES; DR. WATTS; DR. MCCLEAVE; DR. RON WOODALL; LIEUTENANT "UNKNOWN" BONNER; CAPTAIN UNKNOWN DAVIS;EMIL DANEFF; WEXFORD HEALTH SOURCES, INC.; JOHN DOE, I, CEO of Correctional Medical Services; JOHN DOE, II, CEO of Wexford Health Sources, Inc.; JASON HOLMES; HUBERT DAVIS; RITA BONNER; CAPTAIN PAGE; CAPTAIN ENLERS; CAPTAIN SIMMS; BRENDA SIMMS; NINA ENLERS; SHARON PAIGE, Defendants-Appellees No. 09-60959 UNITED STATES COURT OF APPEALS FOR THE FIFTH CIRCUIT

For BOBBY KING, JOHN DOE, I, CEO of Correctional Medical Services, ARNOLD, Doctor, RUTHIE HALL, Nurse, Defendants - Appellees: Robert H. Pedersen, Watkins & Eager, P.L.L.C., Jackson, MS.For BEARRY, Doctor, WATTS, Doctor, WALKER, Doctor, Defendants - Appellees: Robert H. Pedersen, Watkins & Eager, P.L.L.C., Jackson, MS; Vardaman Kimball Smith, III, Bryan Nelson, P.A., Hattiesburg, MS.For MILLIS WASHINGTON, MCCLEAVE, Doctor, Defendants - Appellees: Joseph A. O'Connell, III, Esq., Vardaman

Kimball Smith, III, Bryan Nelson, P.A., Hattiesburg, MS.For RON WOODALL, WEXFORD HEALTH SOURCES INC, EMIL DANEFF, Defendants - Appellees: Joseph A. O'Connell, III, Esq., Bryan Nelson, P.A., Hattiesburg, MS. Concealed evidence they deny/delay treatment for serious medical needs. They examine the patient but do not follow community standards to ensure treatment is effective. They have retained staff who issue whatever declaration/expert report is necessary to defeat claims

S. JOHN ASHLEY HALE, Plaintiff--Appellant, v. RONALD KING, Superintendent of Southern Mississippi Correctional Institution; MARGARET BINGHAM, Superintendent of Southern Mississippi Correctional Institution; CHRISTOPHER EPPS, Commissioner of Mississippi Department of Corrections; MIKE HATTEN, Health Service Administrator of Wexford for Southern Mississippi Correctional Institution; JOHN DOE, Physician at Southern Mississippi Correctional Institution; DOCTOR ZANDU, Psychiatrist at Central Mississippi Correctional Facility; DOCTOR PATRICK ARNOLD, Physician for Correctional Medical Services at Southern Mississippi Correctional Institution; DOCTOR WILLIAMS, Psychiatrist of Correctional Medical Services for Southern Mississippi Correctional Institution; DOCTOR TRINCA, Physician for Wexford at Southern Mississippi Correctional Institution; MIRIAM MOULDS, Kitchen Supervisor at Southern Mississippi Correctional Institution; JOHN DOE 2, Chief Executive Officer of Correctional Medical Services for Mississippi Department of Corrections; JOHN DOE 3, Chief Executive Officer of Wexford at Southern Mississippi Correctional Institution for Mississippi Department of Corrections; DOCTOR MCCLEAVE; DOCTOR WOODALL; WEXFORD HEALTH SERVICES, Defendants--Appellees. No. 07-60997 UNITED STATES COURT OF APPEALS FOR THE FIFTH CIRCUIT

For PATRICK ARNOLD, Physician for Correctional Medical Services at Southern Mississippi Correctional Institution, Defendant - Appellee: Katie Lofton Wallace, Brunini, Grantham, Grower & Hewes, P.L.L.C., Jackson, MS. For TRINCA, Physician for Wexford at Southern Mississippi Correctional Institution, MCCLEAVE, WOODALL, WEXFORD HEALTH SERVICES, Defendants - Appellees: Joseph A. O'Connell, III, Esq., Vardaman Kimball Smith, III, Bryan Nelson, P.A., Hattiesburg, MS. . Concealed evidence they deny/delay treatment for serious medical needs such as chronic Hepatitis C, chronic back problems, and psychiatric conditions They examine the patient but do not follow community standards to ensure treatment is effective. They have retained staff who issue whatever declaration/expert report is necessary to defeat claims

T. OSVALDO C. PALAZON, RONNIE E. CONNOLLY, COLLINS MURRAY, RICARDO PEREZ, WILLIAM BISHOP, WILLIE JONES, AARON KOSBERG, DANIEL MAGLIO, AUSTIN SPEAS, Plaintiffs, KENNETH MCKENNA, Plaintiff-Appellant, versus SECRETARY FOR THE DEPARTMENT OF CORRECTIONS, WEXFORD HEALTH SOURCES INC., DR. HARIDAS NARSI BHADJA, DENISE KELCHNER, Defendants-Appellees, FLORIDA CORRECTIONAL MEDICAL AUTHORITY, Defendant. No. 07-14451 UNITED STATES COURT OF APPEALS FOR THE ELEVENTH CIRCUIT

For Wexford Health Sources Inc., Haridas Bhadja, Dr., Appellees: Mitchel Chusid, Ritter Chusid Bivona & Cohen, LLP, CORAL SPRINGS, FL.For Denise Kelchner, Appellee: Mitchel Chusid, Ritter Chusid Bivona & Cohen, LLP, CORAL SPRINGS, FL; Charles T. Whitelock, Whitelock & Associates, FORT LAUDERDALE, FL. . . Concealed evidence they deny/delay treatment for serious medical needs such as hernia. They examine the patient but do not follow community standards to ensure treatment is effective. They have retained staff who issue whatever declaration/expert report is necessary to defeat claims

U. CHARLES ISELEY, Appellant v. JEFFREY BEARD; ROBERT BITNER; KENNETH KYLER; FRANK GILLIS; WILMA SEWELL; KANDIS DASCANI; JOSEPH KORT, DIANA BANEY; PATRICIA EVERHART; PATRICIA YARGER; DAWN MILLS, Physician Asst.; PAUL ROEMER; MARY SHOWALTER; KILE; CYNTHIA STEVENS; JOHN SIDLER; PHS, INC.; ASG, INC.; WEXFORD

HEALTH SERVICES, INC. NO. 06-2465 UNITED STATES COURT OF APPEALS FOR THE THIRD CIRCUIT

For DAWN MILLS, PAUL ROEMER, WEXFORD HEALTH SER, Appellees: Samuel H. Foreman, Weber, Gallagher, Simpsons, Stapleton, Fires & Newby, Pittsburgh, PA. . Concealed evidence they deny/delay treatment for serious medical needs such as including Hepatitis-C ("HCV"), fibromyalgia, chronic fatigue syndrome, and rheumatoid arthritis. They examine the patient but do not follow community standards to ensure treatment is effective. They have retained staff who issue whatever declaration/expert report is necessary to defeat claims

V. SALVATORE CHIMENTI, Appellant v. ROGER KIMBER, Medical Director; BADDICK, Regional Director; ROWE, Wexford Health Sources, Inc.; I. KAUFER, Wexford Health Sources, Inc.; C. POLLOCK, Site Coordinator; FARROHK MOHADJERIN, Former Medical Director; MARTIN F. HORN; ROBERT S. BITNER, Chief Hearing Examiner for the D.O.C.; FREDERICK K. FRANK; PAT YARGER, SCI-Huntingdon Medical Department; P. E. EVERHART, SCI-Huntingdon Medical Department NO. 03-2056 UNITED STATES COURT OF APPEALS FOR THE THIRD CIRCUIT

For PETER BADDICK, Regional Director, ROWE, Wexford Health Sources, Inc., KAUFER, Wexford Health Sources, Inc., POLLOCK, Site Coordinator, FARROHK MOHADJERIN, Dr., Former Medical Director, Appellees: James D. Young, Lavery, Faherty, Young & Patterson, Harrisburg, PA; Patricia L. Dodge, Metz Lewis, Pittsburgh, PA.For MARTIN HORN, ROBERT BITNER, Chief Hearing Examiner for the D.O.C., FREDERICK FRANK, PATRICIA YARGER, SCI-Huntingdon Medical Department, PATRICIA EVERHART, SCI-Huntingdon Medical Department, Appellees: John J. Talaber, Pennsylvania Department of Corrections, Office of Chief Counsel, Camp Hill, PA. Concealed evidence they deny/delay treatment for serious medical needs such as including Hepatitis-C ("HCV"),.. They have retained staff who issue whatever declaration/expert report is necessary to defeat claims

W. LEONARD T. WILLIAMSON, Appellant v. WEXFORD HEALTH SOURCES, INC.; STATE CORRECTIONAL INSTITUTION, at Pittsburgh (SCIP) Medical Department; DON GEORGE, RN; BONNIE BELL, RN; RACHELLE, RN; NOEL RANKIN, RN; MARSHA HANCOCK, RN; TOM MCDONOUGH, PHYSICIANS ASSISTANT NO. 04-3481 UNITED STATES COURT OF APPEALS FOR THE THIRD CIRCUIT

For WEXFORD HEALTH SER, Appellee: Samuel H. Foreman, Weber, Gallagher, Simpson, Stapleton, Fires & Newby, Pittsburgh, PA. Concealed evidence there are no available remedies under PLRA as grievance staff have been directed not to grant relief They have retained staff who issue whatever declaration/expert report is necessary to defeat claims

X. RODERIC R. McDOWELL, Plaintiff-Appellant, versus PERNELL BROWN, JOHN DOE, No. 1 WEXFORD HEALTH SOURCES, INC., et al., Defendants-Appellees. No. 04-10272 UNITED STATES COURT OF APPEALS FOR THE ELEVENTH CIRCUIT

For Brown, Pernell, Doe, John, Wexford Health Sources, Inc., ABC Corporation, DEF Corporation, GHA Corporation, JKL Corporation, Appellees: Johnson, Deana Simon, Cruser & Mitchell, LLP, Norcross, GA. Concealed evidence they delay/deny treatment often causing paralysis.

Y. Robert P. Torres, Plaintiff, vs. Charles Ryan, et al., Defendants.No. CV 12-0006-PHX-JAT (DKD)UNITED STATES DISTRICT COURT FOR THE DISTRICT OF ARIZONA

For Charles L Ryan, Named as Charles Ryan, ADOC Director, Defendant: Ashley Brook Zuerlein, LEAD ATTORNEY, Office of the Attorney General - Phoenix, Phoenix, AZ; Michael Evan Gottfried, LEAD AT-

TORNEY, Office of the Attorney General, Phoenix, AZ. For Dora B Schriro, Former ADOC Director, Robert Jones, M.D., Dennis R Kendall, Medical Programs Director, Defendants: Michael Evan Gottfried, LEAD ATTORNEY, Office of the Attorney General, Phoenix, AZ.For Unknown Lewis, M.D., Unknown Echeverria, M.D., Defendants: Brandi Christine Blair, Edward G Hochuli, LEAD ATTORNEYS, Jones Skelton & Hochuli PLC, Phoenix, AZ. Concealed evidence they deny/delay treatment his Hepatitis C. They have retained staff who issue whatever declaration/expert report is necessary to defeat claims.

Z. Galen Lloyd Houser, Plaintiff -vs- Charles L. Ryan, et al., Defendants.CV-13-0200-PHX-GMS (JFM)UNITED STATES DISTRICT COURT FOR THE DISTRICT OF ARIZONA

Brandi Christine Blair, Edward G Hochuli, LEAD ATTORNEYS, Jones Skelton & Hochuli PLC, Phoenix, AZ. Concealed evidence they deny/delay treatment for migraines, moderate to severe psoriasis, psoriatic arthritis, chronic lower back pain due to disc degeneration, and acid reflux.. They have retained staff who issue whatever declaration/expert report is necessary to defeat claims.

<u>THE POLICY AT ISSUE</u>

In the above example the allegation should be something like this:

> Samuel H. Foreman, Esq., Leah M. Lewis, Esq., Weber, Gallagher, & Newby, Simpson, Stapleton, Fires PA.has implemented the custom and tradition in
> Which members of his firm perpetrate fraud upon the court
> to prevail in litigation.   Specifically they conceal evidence,
> manufacture evidence and submit false declarations to improperly
> influence the courts in their decisions. This unconscionable plan
> has employees such as retained counsel in other states and others set
> forth in this complaint, among others, perpetrate fraud upon the court."

<u>ROUTINE FAILURE TO FOLLOW RULES OF THE COURT IN DISCOVERY AND LITIGATION</u>

Redman v County Of San Diego, 942 F.2d 1435, 1445 (9th Cir. 1991)(en banc) states routine failure to follow written rules hold the defendants liable. Defendants, and each of them, as discussed above routinely fail to follow the provisions of Federal Rules Of Civil Procedure 26 through 37 pursuant to their unconscionable scheme to influence the courts.

<u>IMPACT OF THEIR ACTION</u>

As a direct consequence of their failure plaintiff did not prevail in the litigation. But for their actions plaintiff would have prevailed.

<u>RELIEF REQUESTED</u>

Plaintiff demands a trial by jury, damages and for an order declaring the judgment void due to fraud upon the court, costs, fees and such other relief as the court may deem fit and proper.

<u>RACKETEERING ACTION</u>

Title IX Of The Organized Crime Control Act Of 1990 (OCCA) Public Law No. 91-452 Stat. 941 (1970) codified at 18 U.S.C. 1961 etc. seq., the Racketeer Influenced and Corrupt Organizations Act aka RICO is a "stealth litigation weapon which Miranda v Ponce Fed. Bank, 948 F.2d 41, 44 (1st Cir. 1991) describes "as an unusually potent weapon---the litigation equivalent of the thermonuclear device." When businesses entities and litigants such as Corizon Inc and Wexford Health Sources engage in litigation fraud with impunity, there is no reason why this "stealth" weapon cannot be used against them.

In Living Designs Inc., et al., v   E.I.DuPont De Nemours And Company, et. Al., 431 F.3d 353 (9th Cir. 2005)

DuPont fraudulently induced the settlement of a product liability litigation by not disclosing in discovery that Benlate was contaminated with SU's. The Ninth Circuit stated reliance was not necessary to prove fraud and that RICO claims may be filed.

Corizon and Wexford do just that and may be sued under RICO.

STATUTES OF LIMITATIONS

The Court in Living Designs Inc., et al., v E.I.DuPont De Nemours And Company, et. Al., 431 F.3d 353 (9th Cir. 2005) states "The limitations period for civil RICO actions begins to run when a plaintiff knows or should know of the injury which is a basis for the action" RICO has a four year statute of limitations and its "tail" makes 10 year old racketeering acts part of the pattern of racketeering activity, thereby expanding the scope of the relevant events.

JURISDICION AND VENUE

A civil RICO may be brought "against any person" in any federal or state court in the United States "in which the person resides, is found has an agent or transacts his affairs" 18 U.S.C. 1965(a). When "the ends of justice require a lawsuit against businesses, such as Corizon or Wexford can be filed in any state or federal court they have conducted business in, including states where their contracts were terminate. Tafflin v Levitt, 493 U.S. 455 (1990) When "the ends of justice require a lawsuit against businesses, such as Corizon or Wexford can be filed in any state or federal court they have conducted business in, including states where their contracts were terminate. Tafflin v Levitt, 493 U.S. 455 (1990)

PARTIES

18 U.S.C. 1961(3) provides a" person includes any individual or entity capable of holding a legal or beneficial interest in property" This is an essential allegation.

ENTERPRISE

18 U.S.C. 1961(4) requires an enterprise different and distinct from defendant Cedric Kushner Promotions Ltd. Vs. King, 533 U.S. 158, 161 (2001). It can be made of " any individual, partnership, corporation, association, or other legal entity, and any union or group of individuals associated in fact although not a legal entity." Engaged in and the activities of which affect interstate commerce. Living Designs stated the lawyers for DuPont with DuPont can be the enterprise. Lawyers for Corizon/Wexford with Corizon/Wexford can be the enterprise..

CONTINUOUS PLUS

> "Focusing on the "continuity plus relationship" requirement explained in Sedima, we have noted that a determination as to whether "a pattern of racketeering activity exists in any given situation is a Fact-specific situation hinging on a variety of relevant factors. Jones v Lampe, 845 F.2d, 755, 757 (7th Cir. 1988) These factors include: (1) the number and variety of the predicate acts and the length of time over which they were committed; (2) the number of victims; (3) the presence of separate schemes; and (4) the occurrence of distinct injuries."

Gagan v American cablevision, Inc., 77 F.3d 951, 962-963 (7th Cir. 1996) The Seventh Circuit determined that though Gagan was the only limited partner "victimized by the Falcon sale and diversion of proceeds" "limited partners who sold their interests were also victimized."

RICO CONSPIRACY

18 U.S.C. 1962(d) makes it illegal "for any person to conspire to violate" subparts (a)(b)or (c) of 18 U.S.C. 1962 This according to Reeves v Ernest Young, 507 U.S. 170 (1993) means a person who does not actually violate 18 U.S.C. 1962(a)(b) or (c) is liable as 18 U.SC. 1962(d) is no "coterminous with liability" under 18 U.S.C. 1962 ()(b) or (c) United States v Qunitanilla, 2 F.3d 1469, 1485 (7th Cir. 1993)

REMEDY AND REDEMPTION

The court in MCM Partners Inc v Andrews-Bartlett & Assoc. Inc, 62 F.3d 967 (7th Cir. 1995) stated the defendant "need not have agreed to actually commit the predicate acts" "or even those acts so long as (they) agreed that the acts would be committed on behalf of the conspiracy." City Of Vernon v Southern Cal. Edison. Co. 955 F.2d 1361, 1371 (9th Cir. 1992)

This would allow Corizon/Wexford nurses, grievance staff, providers, attorneys to be named as defendants.

GOVERNMENT PROCESSES

Corizon/Wexford employees/agents buy meals and give other gifts to state authorities. This buying of meals/gifts can hold them liable.

In Mylan Lab Inc v Matkari, 7 F.3d 1130 (4th Cir.1993) to "undermine the integrity of the FDA approval process in order to improperly obtain economic advantage" 1134 Mylan staff paid for "five meals" to FDA officials over a two year period. The Third Circuit upheld the wire fraud and mail fraud predicates based on the submission of false ANDAs to FDA and FDA relying on these to approve and FDA mailed to Mylan and "also mailed to corporate defendants confidential information submitted by Mylan in order to further facilitate the approval." 1137.

Corizon lobbied through former ADOC Director Terry Stewart and Medical Director Thomas Lutz to obtain the contracts. Both Corizon and Wexford promised ADOC employees and hired them after the contracts were awarded. They submit reports by wire and mail which incorrectly show they are providing care that the contracts allow, when as a matter of fact, they are not.

During litigation their lawyers transmit by e.mail and mail documents to Corizon/Wexford employees.

To interfere with the judicial process they transmit by mail and wire discovery requests/responses , declarations and they also send these to the courts.

INJURY

Living Designs states :
"The financial loss Plaintiffs claim is that they settled their claims for a smaller percentage of their alleged damages than they could have received absent DuPont's fraudulent inducement"

So the amount one could have received as settlement is the injury.

IMMUNE LITIGATION CONDUCT

Living Designs states "the RICO statute itself provides that conduct relating to prior litigation may constitute racketeering activity." As such the conduct in prior litigation is subject to RICO.

PATTERN OF RACKETEERING ACTIVITY

The complaint must state "defendants and each of them committed at least two acts of racketeering activity one of which occurred after October 15, 1970 and the last act within ten years of the prior act of racketeering."

SAMPLE COMPLAINT AGAINST CORIZON

PARTIES

1. John Kristoffer Larsgard, Plaintiff, vs. Corizon Health, Inc., and DOES ONE TO TEN Defendants.Defendants and each of them are persons capable of holding a legal or beneficial interest in property" 18 U.S.C. 1961(3)

BACKGROUND

REMEDY AND REDEMPTION

2. In John Kristoffer Larsgard, Plaintiff, vs. Corizon Health, Inc., Defendant.No. CV 13-01747-PHX-SPL (JFM) UNITED STATES DISTRICT COURT FOR THE DISTRICT OF ARIZONA (APPENDIX C)   defendant submitted false discovery showing It delays/denies consult requests,   post-op x-rays , x-ray and imagings , treatment for cervical fusion surgery , for return for follow up;   attempts to wean off of the medication that is effective per its policy causing inmates;   to suffer severe bouts of pain resulting in unfavorable settlement.

JURISDICTION AND VENUE

3. Corizon   transacts its   affairs in this district, hence jurisdiction is proper.   18 U.S.C. 1965(a).

ENTERPRISE

4. Corizon Health Incorporated, a Delaware Corporation, Heather Alexander Neal, Joseph Scott Conlon, William W Drury, Jr., Renaud Cook Drury Mesaros   PA, is the associated in fact enterprise   "THE RENAUD COOK ENTERPRISE " different and distinct from defendant   engaged in and the activities of which affect interstate commerce 18 U.S.C. 1961(4) These fraudulent acts are not isolated but part of a fraudulent pattern of conduct made of hundreds of fraudulent predicate acts, engaged in by defendant, in order to defeat claims and awards.

5. As a direct and proximate cause of defendant's conduct, of the pattern of racketeering activity, plaintiff and other litigants suffered damages to their property.

6. One of the purposes and functions of the enterprise is to engage in the legitimate business of health care and defending lawsuits. The illegitimate business of the enterprise is to perpetrate fraud, conceal   evidence, manufacture evidence, defeat valid claims, awards. Defendant knowingly and willfully associated with the enterprise, and conducted and participated in its affairs, directly and/or indirectly, by the predicate acts, acts of racketeering alleged in the complaint violating 18 U.S.C. 1962©. It did so by the use of mails and wires violating 18 U.S.C. 1341, 1331 which is racketeering activity in 18 U.S.C. 1961(1)(B).

7. *Defendant authorized, requested, commanded, ratified, recklessly tolerated the unlawful conduct. It did so as a director, high management agent, acquiring or maintaining an interest in the business and profits of the enterprise , in furtherance of the business and activities of the enterprise.*

8. *Defendant conspired with members of the enterprise to violate 18 U.S.C. 1962(a)(b)(c)*

Defendant violated 18 U.S.C. 1962(a)(b)(c)(d).

CONTINUOUS PLUS

9. The following acts show a continuity plus relationship.   The RICO statute itself provides that conduct relating to prior litigation may constitute racketeering activity.

PATTERN OF RACKETEERING ACTIVITY

10. Defendants committed at least two acts of racketeering activity one of which occurred after October 15, 1970 and the last act within ten years of the prior act of racketeering through the associated in fact enterprise. They used the United States Mail and wires to engage in this conduct. *These fraudulent acts are not isolated but part of a fraudulent pattern of conduct made of hundreds of fraudulent predicate acts, engaged in by defendant, in order to defeat claims and awards.*

REMEDY AND REDEMPTION

A. In John Kristoffer Larsgard, Plaintiff, vs. Corizon Health, Inc., Defendant.No. CV 13-01747-PHX-SPL (JFM) UNITED STATES DISTRICT COURT FOR THE DISTRICT OF ARIZONA (APPENDIX C)

Defendant submitted false discovery showing It delays/denies consult requests, post-op x-rays, x-ray and imagings, treatment for cervical fusion surgery, for return for follow up; attempts to wean off of the medication that is effective per its policy causing inmates; to suffer severe bouts of pain resulting in unfavorable settlement.

B. Kevin Mitchell, Plaintiff, v. Corizon Health, Inc., et al., Defendants. No. CV 14-1754-PHX-DGC (BSB)UNITED STATES DISTRICT COURT FOR THE DISTRICT OF ARIZONA

Corizon has retained staff who issue whatever declaration/expert report is necessary to defeat claims. Through counsel who have first hand knowledge through information gained through prior litigation For Corizon Health Incorporated, a Tennessee corporation, State of Arizona, a governmental entity, Defendant: Joseph Scott Conlon, LEAD ATTORNEY, Renaud Cook Drury Mesaros PA, Phoenix, AZ. Concealed evidence that all around the nation there are too many complaints that Corizon has been unwilling to appropriately staff prisons with sufficient and competent health care providers

C. Thomas Bartholomew Layden, IV, Plaintiff, v. Charles L. Ryan, Corizon Incorporated, Michael Hegmann, Subodh Shroff, Alison Scott, Matthew Musson, Richard Pratt, Kamal Rastogi, Defendants. No. CV 14-02470 PHX DJH (DMF) UNITED STATES DISTRICT COURT FOR THE DISTRICT OF ARIZONA

Corizon has retained staff who issue whatever declaration/expert report is necessary to defeat claims. Through counsel who have first hand knowledge through information gained through prior litigation For Subodh Shroff, Doctor at Meadows Unit, Alison Scott, Nurse Supervisor at Meadows Unit, Defendants: Joseph Scott Conlon, LEAD ATTORNEY, Renaud Cook Drury Mesaros PA, Phoenix, AZ. It concealed the evidence that there are no available remedies under PLRA for grievance staff have been directed to not afford inmates relief in the grievance process.

D. BETH E. BRONDAS, Plaintiff, v. CORIZON HEALTH, INC., Defendant.CIVIL ACTION NO. 7:14-CV-00369 UNITED STATES DISTRICT COURT FOR THE WESTERN DISTRICT OF VIRGINIA, ROANOKE DIVISION

Corizon working through counsel who have first hand knowledge through information gained through prior litigation For Corizon Health, Inc., Defendant: Edward J. McNelis, III, Elizabeth Martin Muldowney, LEAD ATTORNEYS, Rawls McNelis Mitchell, Richmond, VA .concealed evidence that Corizon's contracts have been repeatedly cancelled for deprivation of adequate medical treatment causing death and permanent injury. It has retained staff who issue whatever declaration/expert report is necessary to defeat claims.

E. JAMES COLEN #604910, Plaintiff, v. CORIZON MEDICAL SERVICES, et al., Defendants.Civil Action No.: 14-12948 UNITED STATES DISTRICT COURT FOR THE EASTERN DISTRICT OF MICHIGAN, SOUTHERN DIVISION

Corizon working through counsel who have first hand knowledge through information gained through prior litigation For Corizon Medical Services, Defendant: Kimberley A. Koester, Christopher Trainor & Associates, White Lake, MI. For Dr Prasad, Rosilyn Jindal, Dr Brady, Dr Suclhir, Dr Martin, Alford, PA, Defendants: Kimberley A. Koester, Christopher Trainor & Associates, White Lake, MI; Ronald W. Chapman, Chapman Law Group, Bloomfield Hills, MI. For A Rogers, RN, Ellenwood, RN, Mary Velarde, RN, Kimmy, RN, Defendants: Allan J. Soros, Michigan Department of Attorney General, Lansing, MI. .concealed evidence that Corizon's has had too many claims stemming from medical care related to injuries sustained; and that administrative remedies are in fact not available because those who administer these have been directed not to afford relief to inmates causing death and permanent injury. It has retained staff who issue whatever declaration/expert report is necessary to defeat claims.

F. MARK FRENCH, Plaintiff, v CORIZON, et al., Defendants Civil Action No. JFM-14-2263 UNITED STATES DISTRICT COURT FOR THE DISTRICT OF MARYLAND

Corizon working through counsel who have first hand knowledge through information gained through prior litigation For Corizon, Defendant: Patricia H Beall, Marks ONeill OBrien Doherty & Kelly PC, Towson, MD.For Dr. Colin Ottey, Ava Joubert, Rebecca Andrews, Rebecca Leatherman, Dianne Harvey, Defendants: Gina Marie Smith, LEAD ATTORNEY, Meyers Rodbell and Rosenbaum PA, Riverdale, MD; Patricia H Beall, Marks ONeill OBrien Doherty & Kelly PC, Towson, MD.For Gregg L. Hershberger, Warden Frank Bishup, Defendants: Thomas E Dernoga, LEAD ATTORNEY, Office of the Attorney General, Baltimore, MD. Concealed evidence that they as a matter of practice routinely deny appropriate medical treatment for hepatitis C. causing death. It has retained staff who issue whatever declaration/expert report is necessary to defeat claims.

G. IVES T. ARTIS, Plaintiff, vs. BYUNGHAK JIN, Medical Director (indiviaul Compasity); CORIZON HEALTH, Formerly Prison Healthcare Services (Official Compasity), Defendants. Civil Action No. 13-1226 UNITED STATES DISTRICT COURT FOR THE WESTERN DISTRICT OF PENNSYLVANIA

Corizon working through counsel who have first hand knowledge through information gained through prior litigation For BYUNGHAK JIN (Individaul Compacity), MIN H. PARK, (Individual Compacity), Defendants: J. Eric Barchiesi, LEAD ATTORNEY, Law Offices of Bernard J. Kelly, Pittsburgh, PA. For CORIZON HEALTH, a/k/a PRISON HEALTH CARE SERVICES, Defendant: J. Eric Barchiesi, Law Offices of Bernard J. Kelly, Pittsburgh, PA. concealed evidence they routinely deny treatment for ankle injury , there are too many such incidents and the administrative remedies are not available in fact within the meaning of PLRA for grievance staff have been directed not to afford relief. It has retained staff who issue whatever declaration/expert report is necessary to defeat claims.

H. Ardra Young, Plaintiff, v. LaToya Jackson, Vindha Jayawardena, Michigan Department of Corrections, and Corizon Health, Inc., Defendants.Case No. 12-cv-12751 UNITED STATES DISTRICT COURT FOR THE EASTERN DISTRICT OF MICHIGAN, SOUTHERN DIVISION

Corizon working through counsel who have first hand knowledge through information gained through prior litigation For Prison Healthcare Services, Inc, Defendant: Kimberley A. Koester, Ronald W. Chapman, Chapman Law Group, Bloomfield Hills, MI. concealed evidence there are too many incidents where they have not properly treated inuries and they conceal this evidence of other acts as a matter of practice as they show they have implemented a policy, custom, or practice It has retained staff who issue whatever declaration/expert report is necessary to defeat claims.

I. WILLIAM R. TUBBS, PLAINTIFF ADC # 120585, v. CORIZON, INC.; et al., DEFENDANTS 5:13CV00377-BSM-JJV UNITED STATES DISTRICT COURT FOR THE EASTERN DISTRICT OF ARKANSAS, PINE BLUFF DIVISION

Corizon working through counsel who have first hand knowledge through information gained through prior litigation For Corizon Inc, Estella Bland, ANP, Laura Morgan, RN, A Pevey, Annette Esaw, Medical Records, Cummins Unit, ADC, Rice, Former Employee (Nurse), Cummins Unit, ADC, Defendants: Michelle Banks Odum, LEAD ATTORNEY, Humphries, Odum & Eubanks, White Hall, AR. For Crystal Woods, Classification Officer, Cummins Unit, ADC, Mark Warner, Former Assistant Warden, Cummins Unit, ADC (originally named as Warner), Rory Griffin, originally identified as "Roy Griffin", Wendy Kelly, Deputy Director of Medical Services, ADC, Gaylon Lay, Warden, Cummins Unit,

ADC, Debra Glover, Garment Factory Supervisor, Cummins Unit, ADC, Danny Burl, Warden, East Arkansas Unit, Stewart, Captain, East Arkansas Unit, Marion Beard, Captain, East Arkansas Unit (originally named as Baird), Paulette Green-Davis, Originally named as John Doe, Defendants: Nga Mahfouz, LEAD ATTORNEY, Arkansas Attorney General's Office, Little Rock, AR. concealed evidence of the fact that when inmates compel them to provide treatment they do all possible to ensure the recovery is painful and if possible there is permanent injury. It has retained staff who issue whatever declaration/expert report is necessary to defeat claims.

J. KENNETH R. HARRISON, #160623, Plaintiff, v. CORIZON MEDICAL SERVICES, Defendant.CIVIL ACTION NO. 2:14-CV-1251-MHTUNITED STATES DISTRICT COURT FOR THE MIDDLE DISTRICT OF ALABAMA, EASTERN DIVISION

Corizon through counsel who have first hand knowledge through information gained through prior litigation For Corizon Medical Services, Defendant: William Richard Lunsford, LEAD ATTORNEY, Maynard Cooper & Gale PC, Huntsville, AL. concealed evidence they have a well documented history of delaying/denying treatment for heart condition and that there are no available administrative remedies within the meaning of PLRA because as a matter of routine though who handle grievances do not afford relief. It has retained staff who issue whatever declaration/expert report is necessary to defeat claims.

K. JANET MOSELY, et al., Plaintiffs, v. STATE OF MISSOURI; CORIZON, INC.; IAN WALLACE; TRAVIS WILHITE; and DONNA SPAVEN, Defendants Case No. 1:15CV00052 AGF UNITED STATES DISTRICT COURT FOR THE EASTERN DISTRICT OF MISSOURI, SOUTHEASTERN DIVISION

Corizon through counsel who have first hand knowledge through information gained through prior litigation For State of Missouri, Ian Wallace, Travis Wilhite, Defendants: Dana W. Tucker, LEAD ATTORNEY, ATTORNEY GENERAL OF MISSOURI, St. Louis, MO. For Corizon, Inc., Donna Spaven, Defendants: J. Thaddeus Eckenrode, LEAD ATTORNEY, ECKENRODE-MAUPIN, St. Louis, MO. Concealed evidence of the fact that pursuant to its policies Corizon does not notify prison officials of inmate serious medical conditions that may cause their death or permanent injury and because of this the death. It concealed the other similar incidents. It has retained staff who issue whatever declaration/expert report is necessary to defeat claims.

L. MAURICE D. HARPER, Plaintiff, v. CORIZON, LOUIS GIORLA, MICHELLE FARRELL, FRANK ABELLO, MARIEL TRIMBLE, and PANTAL JEAN, Defendants. CIVIL ACTION No. 14-639 UNITED STATES DISTRICT COURT FOR THE EASTERN DISTRICT OF PENNSYLVANIA

Corizon through counsel who have first hand knowledge through information gained through prior litigation For CORIZON, LOUIS GIORLA, MICHELE FARRELL, FRANK ABELLO, MARIEL TRIMBLE, Defendants: STEPHEN E. SIEGRIST, LEAD ATTORNEY, O'CONNOR KIMBALL, LLP, PHILADELPHIA, PA. concealed evidence of the fact that nationwide there are too many complaints of it ignoring serious medical needs regarding severe acid reflux disease ith inmates being permanently injured. It has retained staff who issue whatever declaration/expert report is necessary to defeat claims.

M. DEREK JOHNSON, personal representative of KELLY CONRAD GREEN II, deceased; KELLY CONRAD GREEN and SANDY PULVER, Plaintiffs, v. CORIZON HEALTH, INC., a Tennessee Corporation; LANE COUNTY, an Oregon county; DR. CARL KELDIE, an individual; DR. JUSTIN MONTOYA, an individual; VICKI THOMAS, an individual; KIRSTIN WHITE, an individual;; SHARON EPPERSON (nee FAGAN), an individual, and JACOB PLEICH, an individual, Defendants. 6:13-cv-1855-TC UNITED STATES DISTRICT COURT FOR THE DISTRICT OF OREGON

REMEDY AND REDEMPTION

Corizon through counsel who have first hand knowledge through information gained through prior litigation For Kelly Conrad Green, Sandy Pulver, Plaintiffs: John T. Devlin, LEAD ATTORNEY, Elden M. Rosenthal, Rosenthal & Greene, P.C., Portland, OR.For Derek Johnson, as personal representative of Kelly Conrad Green II, deceased, Plaintiff: Elden M. Rosenthal, John T. Devlin, LEAD ATTORNEYS, Rosenthal & Greene, P.C., Portland, OR.For Corizon Health, Inc., a Tennessee corporation, Dr. Carl Keldie, an individual, Dr. Justin Montoya, an individual, Vicki Thomas, an individual, Kirstin White, an individual, Jacob Pleich, an individual, Sharon Epperson, an individual born Sharon Fagan, Defendants: James M. Daigle, LEAD ATTORNEY, Robert B. Coleman, Stewart Sokol & Larkin LLC, Portland, OR.For Lane County, an Oregon county, Defendant: Sebastian Tapia, LEAD ATTORNEY, Lane County Counsel, Eugene, OR.Concealed evidence there are too many complaints that it fails to failed to perform reasonably necessary medical examination and transporting inmates without taking measures to stabilize their neck or spine with too many inmtes left incontinent and unmoving quadriplegic very often killing the inmate. It has retained staff who issue whatever declaration/expert report is necessary to defeat claims.

N. DAVID WILSON, PLAINTIFF VS. DON NELSON, CORIZON LLC, JAMES PRATT, JOHN HAROLD AND JIM McLEAN, DEFENDANTS CASE NO. 6:13-CV-6036 UNITED STATES DISTRICT COURT FOR THE WESTERN DISTRICT OF ARKANSAS, HOT SPRINGS DIVISION

Corizon through counsel who have first hand knowledge through information gained through prior litigation For Don Nelson, Ouachita River Unit, ADC, John Harold, Construction Supervisor, Ouachita River Unit, ADC, Jim McLean, Construction Supervisor, Ouachita River Unit, ADC, Defendants: Jonathan Q. Warren, LEAD ATTORNEY, Arkansas Attorney General's Office, Little Rock, AR. For Corizon, James Pratt, Health Care Administrator, Corizon, Defendants: Michelle Banks Odum, LEAD ATTORNEY, Humphries & Lewis, White Hall, AR. Concealed evidence that nationwide it has too many complaints that it delays/denies treatment after injuries and that there are no available remedies within the meaning of PLRA for grievance staff have been directed not to afford relief. It has retained staff who issue whatever declaration/expert report is necessary to defeat claims.

O. SCOTT RICHARD HANSON, Plaintiffs, v. JOHANNA SMITH, DR. SCOTT DAVID LOSSMAN; DR. APRIL CHARLENE DAWSON; DR. MYUNG AE SONG DO; MS. RONA SIEGERT; JOHN and JANE DOES, One through Ten; CORRECTIONAL MEDICAL SERVICES; and CORIZON MEDICAL SERVICES, Defendants. Case No. 1:11-cv-00525-BLW UNITED STATES DISTRICT COURT FOR THE DISTRICT OF IDAHO

Corizon through counsel who have first hand knowledge through information gained through prior litigation For Scott David Lossman, M.D., April Charlene Dawson, M.D., Myung AE Song Do, M.D., Defendants: John J Burke, Robert Arthur Berry, LEAD ATTORNEYS, ELAM & BURKE, P.A., Boise, ID.For Rona Siegert, Defendant: Leslie Marie Hayes, LEAD ATTORNEY, Idaho Attorney General's Office, Boise, ID; Mark Alan Kubinski, LEAD ATTORNEY, IDAHO DEPT OF CORRECTION, Boise, ID. Concealed evidence that nationwide it has too many incidents of deficient care in the diagnosis and treatment of his prostate cancer with inmates experiencing difficulty urinating and very often due to these delays inmates have died and/or their conditions not correctable. It has retained staff who issue whatever declaration/expert report is necessary to defeat claims.

P. THOMAS EDWARD JONES, #140289, Plaintiff, v. CORIZON, et al., Defendants.CASE NO. 2:12-CV-786-WHA [WO]UNITED STATES DISTRICT COURT FOR THE MIDDLE DISTRICT OF ALABAMA, NORTHERN DIVISION

Corizon through counsel who have first hand knowledge through information gained through prior litigation For Corizon, Medical Service Provider, Jean Darbouze, Dr., Ms. Wilson, Director of Nursing,

Mrs. Edward, Chronic Care Nurse, Defendants: Philip Guy Piggott, LEAD ATTORNEY, Starnes Davis Florie LLP, Birmingham, AL. concealed evidence that there are too many incidents where it has denied treatment for sinusitis, loss of vision gastrointestinal issues causing permanent injury. It has retained staff who issue whatever declaration/expert report is necessary to defeat claims.

Q. JAMES A. DULAK, Plaintiff, v. CORIZON INC., Dr. HUTCHINSON, Dr. STIEVE, Dr. ABDEL-LATIF, PA JINDAHL, ROGERS, TAMMY ROTHHAAR, Defendants. Case No. 14-10193 UNITED STATES DISTRICT COURT FOR THE EASTERN DISTRICT OF MICHIGAN, SOUTHERN DIVISION

Through counsel who have first hand knowledge through information gained through prior litigation For Hutchinson, Dr, Abdellatif, Dr, Defendants: Kimberley A. Koester, Ronald W. Chapman, Chapman Law Group, Bloomfield Hills, MI.For Steve, Dr, Defendant: Allan J. Soros, Michigan Department of Attorney General, Corrections Division, Lansing, MI. Corizon concealed evidence it refuses to treat neuropathy, by medication that is effective providing treatment that does not relieve the pain. It has retained staff who issue whatever declaration/expert report is necessary to defeat claims.

R. TERRY DAVIS, Plaintiff, v. CORIZON, et al., Defendants. Case No. 5:13-cv-0949-CLS-TMP UNITED STATES DISTRICT COURT FOR THE NORTHERN DISTRICT OF ALABAMA, NORTHEASTERN DIVISION

Corizon through counsel who have first hand knowledge through information gained through prior litigation For Corizon, C.M.S., Dr Stubbs, Dr Barrett, D Hunt, Defendants: Philip G Piggott, STARNES DAVIS FLORIE LLP, Birmingham, AL. concealed evidence that it denied/delays treatment of back pain, fracture or dislocation, and an impression, osteoarthritis or bone spurs providing treatment hat is not effective. It has retained staff who issue whatever declaration/expert report is necessary to defeat claims.

S. CHRISTOPHER LEWIS, Plaintiff, v. CORIZON HEALTH CARE, et al., Defendants.CIVIL NO. 4:14-CV-00885 UNITED STATES DISTRICT COURT FOR THE MIDDLE DISTRICT OF PENNSYLVANIA

Through Counsel who have first hand knowledge through information gained through prior litigation For Corizon Health Care, Defendant: Michael C. Mongiello, Marshall Dennehey Warner Coleman and Goggin, Camp Hill, PA. For Bio Reference Labs, Defendant: Jonathan Dryer, Wilson, Elser, Moskowitz, Edelman & Dicker LLP, Philadelphia, PA. concealed evidence that nationwide there are too many complaints that Corizon employees falsify medical records, do not conduct MRI and other tests. It has retained staff who issue whatever declaration/expert report is necessary to defeat claims.

T. EDUARDO OLMEDO, Plaintiff, -against- CORIZON P.C., DR. JEAN RICHARD, and DR. PARK, Defendants. 14 Civ. 3853 (AT)(HBP) UNITED STATES DISTRICT COURT FOR THE SOUTHERN DISTRICT OF NEW YORK

Through Counsel who have first hand knowledge through information gained through prior litigation For Corizon P.C., Defendant: Austa Starr Devlin, Christopher Francis Lyon, Heidell, Pittoni, Murphy & Bach, LLP (NY), New York, NY USA; John Charles O'Brien, Jr., Heidell, Pittoni, Murphy & Bach, LLP (WP), White Plains, NY USA.For Md Jean Richard, Amd Dr. Park, Defendants: Austa Starr Devlin, Christopher Francis Lyon, Heidell, Pittoni, Murphy & Bach, LLP (NY), New York, NY USA. Concealed evidence it denies/delays treatment for physical injury and the necessary therapy until it is too late. It has retained staff who issue whatever declaration/expert report is necessary to defeat claims.

REMEDY AND REDEMPTION

U. CARL RUPERT SMITH, #137 787, Plaintiff, v. CORIZON HEALTH SERVICES, et al., Defendants. CIVIL ACTION NO. 2:15-CV-20-MHT UNITED STATES DISTRICT COURT FOR THE MIDDLE DISTRICT OF ALABAMA, NORTHERN DIVISION

Through Counsel who have first hand knowledge through information gained through prior litigation For Corizon Health Services, Nurse Ellis, Staff Adm., Director of Nursing, in his official and individual capacities, Ms. Copeland, Staff Services Administrator of Health, in her official and individual capacities, Nurse Guice, Staff Nurse Practitioner, in her official and individual capacities, Defendants: William Richard Lunsford, LEAD ATTORNEY, Maynard Cooper & Gale PC, Huntsville, AL. concealed evidence that there are no available administrative remedies under PLRA because those who handle grievances have been directed to refrain from affording relief. It has retained staff who issue whatever declaration/expert report is necessary to defeat claims.

V. CHARLES TONGE, Plaintiff, v. CORIZON HEALTH SERVICES, INC. and THE CITY OF NEW YORK, Defendants. No. 14-CV-3954 (RA) UNITED STATES DISTRICT COURT FOR THE SOUTHERN DISTRICT OF NEW YORK

Through counsel who have first hand knowledge through information gained through prior litigation For Corizon Health Services, Inc., "Corizon", Defendant: John Charles O'Brien , Jr., Heidell, Pittoni, Murphy & Bach, LLP (WP), White Plains, NY. For The City of New York, Defendant: Neil Anthony Giovanatti, LEAD ATTORNEY, New York City Law Department, New York, NY; John Charles O'Brien , Jr., Heidell, Pittoni, Murphy & Bach, LLP (WP), White Plains, NY. Corizon concealed evidence of the fact that nationwide there are too many similar complaints of it not provide treatment that is effective. It has retained staff who issue whatever declaration/expert report is necessary to defeat claims.

W. BRIAN GRIMALDI, Plaintiff, v. CORIZON, INC., f/k/a CORRECTIONAL MEDICAL SERVICES, INC., and ANNIE GREY, Defendants. CIVIL ACTION NO. 10-1686 (JEI/JS) UNITED STATES DISTRICT COURT FOR THE DISTRICT OF NEW JERSEY

Through counsel who have first hand knowledge through information gained through prior litigation For Defendants: Christian M. Scheuerman, Esq., Frances Wang-Deveney, Esq., MARKS, O'NEILL, O'BRIEN, DOHERTY & KELLY, P.C., Pennsauken, Corizon concealed evidence that all through the nation there are too many incidents where inmates who suffer from asthma are not provided proper and timely treatment causing permanent injury and its employees falsify the record. It has retained staff who issue whatever declaration/expert report is necessary to defeat claims.

X. DURWIN C. BOYD (AIS # 189145), Plaintiff, v. CORIZON INC., Defendant. Civil Action No. 2:13CV354-WHA UNITED STATES DISTRICT COURT FOR THE MIDDLE DISTRICT OF ALABAMA, NORTHERN DIVISION

Through counsel who have first hand knowledge through information gained through prior litigation For Corizon, Inc., Defendant: Philip Guy Piggott, LEAD ATTORNEY, Starnes & Atchison, Birmingham, AL. concealed evidence that all around the nation it has the history of delaying/denying treatment for injuries until it is too late. It has retained staff who issue whatever declaration/expert report is necessary to defeat claims.

Y. RUTH DENHAM, as personal representative for the estate of Tracy Lee Veira, Plaintiff, v. CORIZON HEALTH, INC. and VOLUSIA COUNTY, a political subdivision of the State of Florida, Defendants. Case No: 6:13-cv-1425-Orl-40KRS UNITED STATES DISTRICT COURT FOR THE MIDDLE DISTRICT OF FLORIDA, ORLANDO DIVISION

Through Counsel who have first hand knowledge through information gained through prior litigation For Corizon Health, Inc., a Delaware corporation, Defendant: S. Renee Lundy, LEAD ATTORNEY,

Dean, Ringers, Morgan & Lawton, PA, Orlando, FL. For Volusia County, Florida, a political subdivision of the State of Florida, Defendant: Gregg A. Toomey, LEAD ATTORNEY, The Toomey Law Firm LLC, Fort Myers, FL. For Dan H Honeywell, Mediator: James B. Chaplin, LEAD ATTORNEY, Mediation, Inc., Ft Lauderdale, FL. Corizon concealed evidence it provides treatment that is not effective for chronic pain causing death resulted from physiological symptoms caused by opiate withdrawal in certain cases. It has retained staff who issue whatever declaration/expert report is necessary to defeat claims.

Z. JOHN F. WARREN, Plaintiff, v. CORIZON HEALTH; DR. APRIL DAWSON, M.D.; MICHAEL TAKAGI, PA-C; DIANE DICE, PA-C; STEVEN STEDTFELD, PA-C; DAVID FOSS, NP RYAN VALLEY, HASA; BRISTY DELAOE; JOHN DOE PROVIDER; JANE DOE PROVIDER; STEVEN LITTLE, WARDEN; BRENT REINKE, DIRECTOR OF IDAHO DEPT. OF CORRECTIONS; Defendants. Case No. 1:14-CV-00011-EJLUNITED STATES DISTRICT COURT FOR THE DISTRICT OF IDAHO

With the help of counsel who have first hand knowledge through information gained through prior litigation For April Dawson, M.D., Diana Dice, PA-C, Ryan Valley, HSA, Bristy Delaoe, DON, Defendants: John J Burke, LEAD ATTORNEY, ELAM & BURKE, P.A., Boise, ID. Corizon concealed the fact that all around the nation it provides medication that are not effective to manage the conditions at issue. It has retained staff who issue whatever declaration/expert report is necessary to defeat claims.

AA. OSMONDO SMITH, Plaintiff, -against- CORIZON HEALTH SERVICES and THE CITY OF NEW YORK, Defendants. 14 Civ. 08839 (GBD)(SN) UNITED STATES DISTRICT COURT FOR THE SOUTHERN DISTRICT OF NEW YORK

With counsel who have first hand knowledge through information gained through prior litigation For Corizon Health Services, Defendant: John Charles O'Brien, Jr., LEAD ATTORNEY, Heidell, Pittoni, Murphy & Bach,For City of New York, Defendant: Doreen Dufficy, John Charles O'Brien, Jr., Heidell, Pittoni, Murphy & Bach, LLP (WP), White Plains, NY. Corizon concealed evidence that all through the nation its employees are not careful in prescribing medication and in too many cases prescribing ,medication that causes other complications. It has retained staff who issue whatever declaration/expert report is necessary to defeat claims.

BB. STEVE ODOM, Plaintiff, v. CORIZON, INC., et al, Defendants. Case No. 1:14-CV-606 UNITED STATES DISTRICT COURT FOR THE WESTERN DISTRICT OF MICHIGAN, SOUTHERN DIVISION

Through counsel who have first hand knowledge through information gained through prior litigation For Corizon, Inc., Adam M. Edelman, MD, Syed M. Sohail, MD, Bhamini Sudhir, MD, Roger Gerlack, MD, Richard Worel, MD, defendants: Mark D. Lefkow, Nall & Miller LLP, Atlanta, GA; Kimberley A. Koester, Chapman and Associates PC, Bloomfield Hills, MI. For Jeffry C. Stieve, MD, William Borgerding, MD, Unknown Pramstaller, MD, S. Laughhunn, RN, defendants: Robert J. Jenkins, MI Dept Attorney General (Corrections), Corrections Division, Lansing, MI. concealed evidence that there are too many instances that Corizon has denied inmates similar treatment that is effective. It has retained staff who issue whatever declaration/expert report is necessary to defeat claims.

CC. JOHNNY L. McGOWAN, JR., Plaintiff, v. CORIZON MEDICAL, LT. KEVIN GUNN, DR. CLEMENT BARNARD, and DARREL THOMAS, Defendants.No. 3:14-cv-0578UNITED STATES DISTRICT COURT FOR THE MIDDLE DISTRICT OF TENNESSEE, NASHVILLE DIVISION

REMEDY AND REDEMPTION

Through counsel who have first hand knowledge through information gained through prior litigation For Corizon Medical, Dr. Clement Barnard, Darrell Thomas, Defendant: John F. Floyd, Todd & Floyd, PLC, Nashville, TN. For Lt. Kevin Gunn, Lt., Defendant: Pamela S. Lorch, LEAD ATTORNEY, Tennessee Attorney General's Office, Nashville, TN. Corizon concealed evidence that there are too many complaints that it has failed to prescribe adequate pain medication in a timely fashion. It has retained staff who issue whatever declaration/expert report is necessary to defeat claims.

DD. JENNIFER JONES, Plaintiff, v. CORIZON, LLC, et al., Defendants. Case No. 4:15 CV 346 RWSUNITED STATES DISTRICT COURT FOR THE EASTERN DISTRICT OF MISSOURI, EASTERN DIVISION

Through counsel who have first hand knowledge through information gained through prior litigation For Corizon, LLC, Defendant: J. Thaddeus Eckenrode, LEAD ATTORNEY, ECKENRODE-MAUPIN, St. Louis, MO. For St. Louis, Missouri, City of, Paul Geiger, in his individual capacity, Cynthia Siple, in her individual capacity, Alphonso Bratcher, in his individual capacity, Edwin Oluoch, in his individual capacity, James Moss, in his individual capacity, Theresa Smith, in her individual capacity, Dale Glass, in his individual capacity, Defendants: Erin K. McGowan, LEAD ATTORNEY, ST. LOUIS CITY COUNSELOR'S OFFICE, St. Louis, MO. That too many inmates are dying due to their not being given proper care. It has retained staff who issue whatever declaration/expert report is necessary to defeat claims.

EE. DENNIS JAY WARREN, Plaintiff, v. CORIZON HEALTH, et al., Defendants 3:15-cv-00161-JO UNITED STATES DISTRICT COURT FOR THE DISTRICT OF OREGON, PORTLAND DIVISION

Through counsel who have first hand knowledge through information gained through prior litigation For Corizon Health, Subcontracted to Washington County Sheriff Jail, WA.CO. Oregon, Physicians Assistant, PA-C-"Colin", Washington County Jail, Colin Storz, Defendants: James M. Daigle, Stewart Sokol & Larkin LLC, Portland, OR. Concealed evidence that prescribing inappropriate medication is the norm by its employees and too many inmates have been permanently injured and are in pain. It concealed the fact that there are no available remedies under PLRA as staff who handle grievances routinely decline to afford relief. It has retained staff who issue whatever declaration/expert report is necessary to defeat claims.

FF. EARL FARMER, Plaintiff, v. C.L. "BUTCH" OTTER; RANDY BLADES; MS. WAMBLE-FISHER; CATHY STEFFEN; CORIZON MEDICAL SERVICES; IDAHO STATE DEPARTMENT OF CORRECTION; and IDAHO STATE BOARD OF CORRECTION, Defendants. Case No. 1:14-cv-00345-BLW UNITED STATES DISTRICT COURT FOR THE DISTRICT OF IDAHO
Through counsel who have first hand knowledge through information gained through prior litigation For Randy Blades, Wamble-Fisher, Defendants: Phillip J Collaer, LEAD ATTORNEY, ANDERSON JULIAN & HULL, Boise, ID.For Corizon Medical Services, (CMS), Defendant: Dylan Alexander Eaton, J Kevin West, LEAD ATTORNEYS, Parson Behle & Latimer, Boise, ID. It concealed the fact that there are no available remedies under PLRA as staff who handle grievances routinely decline to afford relief. It has retained staff who issue whatever declaration/expert report is necessary to defeat claims.

GG. HAROLD DAVEY CASSELL ADC # 073885, PLAINTIFF v. CORRECT CARE SOLUTIONS, LLC and CORIZON, INC., DEFENDANTS 5:14CV00403-DPM-JJV UNITED STATES DISTRICT COURT FOR THE EASTERN DISTRICT OF ARKANSAS, PINE BLUFF DIVISION

Through counsel who have first hand knowledge through information gained through prior litigation For Harold Davey Cassell, Plaintiff: J. Brooks Wiggins, LEAD ATTORNEY, Attorney at Law, Little Rock, AR Corizon concealed evidence it does delay/deny effective treatment for HEP C AND THERE ARE

REMEDY AND REDEMPTION

TOO MANY SUCH DENIALS. It has retained staff who issue whatever declaration/expert report is necessary to defeat claims.

HH. ROOSEVELT THOMAS, JR., AIS #115280, Plaintiff, vs. CORIZON, INC., Defendant. CIVIL ACTION 15-68-WS-M UNITED STATES DISTRICT COURT FOR THE SOUTHERN DISTRICT OF ALABAMA, SOUTHERN DIVISION

Through counsel who have first hand knowledge through information gained through prior litigation For Corizon, Inc., Defendant: Philip Guy Piggott, LEAD ATTORNEY, Starnes Davis Florie LLP, Birmingham, AL. . Corizon concealed the fact it does delay/deny treatment for fracture until the injury is permanent and there are hundreds of such denials. It has retained staff who issue whatever declaration/expert report is necessary to defeat claims

II. EDWARD E. STEWART, III, Plaintiff, v. MICHAEL WENEROWICZ, DENNIS BRUMFIELD, MICHAEL DOYLE, JOHN HOFER, KEITH VANCLIFF, ROBERT GRUBER, CORIZON HEALTH, INC., RICHARD STEFANIK, M.D., MICHAEL HERBIK, D.O., RAYMOND MARCHAK, P.A., and SUSAN BERRIER, R.N., Defendants. CIVIL ACTION NO. 12-4046 UNITED STATES DISTRICT COURT FOR THE EASTERN DISTRICT OF PENNSYLVANIA

Corizon has retained staff who issue whatever declaration/expert report is necessary to defeat claims. Through counsel who have first hand knowledge through information gained through prior litigation. For EDWARD E. STEWART, III, Plaintiff: HYUNG P. STEELE, ; YVONNE MARIE MCKENZIE, LEAD ATTORNEYS, TANNEIKA MINOTT, PEPPER HAMILTON LLP, PHILADELPHIA, PA; KRYSTEN CONNON, PEPPER HAMILTON, PHILADELPHIA, PA.For RICHARD STEFANIC, M.D., RAY MACHAK, P.A., CORIZON HEALTH INC., Defendants: RASHEEN NICOLE DAVIS, LEAD ATTORNEY, MARSHALL DENNEHEY WARNER COLEMAN & GOGGIN, PHILADELPHIA, PA.For SUSAN BERRIER, R.N., Defendant: KATHY LE, LEAD ATTORNEY, OFFICE OF THE ATTORNEY GENERAL, PHILADELPHIA, PA.For DENNIS BRUMFIELD, MICHAEL DOYLE, JOHN HOFER, KEITH VANCLIFF, ROBERT GRUBER, MICHAEL WENEROWICZ, Defendants: KATHY LE, OFFICE OF THE ATTORNEY GENERAL, PHILADELPHIA, PA. For MICHAEL HERBIK, D.O, Defendant: RASHEEN NICOLE DAVIS, MARSHALL DENNEHEY WARNER COLEMAN & GOGGIN, PHILADELPHIA, PA. They concealed the fact that there are too many instances when physicians are not available to provide treatment and when they examine inmates they fail to conduct thorough examinations.

JJ. CHRISTINA BOBBIN, in her capacity as Plenary Guardian of Carlo Daniel Laudadio, an incapacitated adult, Plaintiff, v. CORIZON HEALTH, INC., NATALIA SAUNDERS, H.S.A., JANICE STEPNOSKI, L.C.S.W., WALTER CARL MORRIS, RN, NOEL DOMINGUEZ, M.D., ANDREW PAUL SAFRON, III, D.O., SVOBODA MARIA HOLT, LMHC, JANET JOAN MEMOLI, RN, MIKE SCOTT, in his official capacity as Lee County Sheriff, PAUL A. PAVESE, Sergeant, and RODNEY K. PAYNE, Deputy, individually, Defendants. Case No: 2:14-cv-158-FtM-29MRM UNITED STATES DISTRICT COURT FOR THE MIDDLE DISTRICT OF FLORIDA, FORT MYERS DIVISION

Corizon has retained staff who issue whatever declaration/expert report is necessary to defeat claims. Through counsel who have first hand knowledge through information gained through prior litigation For Corizon Health, Inc., formerly known as Prison Health Services, Inc., Natalia Saunders, H.S.A., Janice Stepnoski, L.C.S.W., Walter Carl Morris, RN, Noel Dominguez, M.D., Andrew Paul Safron, III, D.O., Janet Joan Memoli, RN, Defendants: Gregg A. Toomey, LEAD ATTORNEY, The Toomey Law Firm LLC, Fort Myers, FL.For Mike Scott, in his official capacity as Lee County Sheriff, Paul A. Pavese, Sergeant, Rodney K. Payne, Deputy, individually, Defendants: Robert C. Shearman, LEAD ATTORNEY, Henderson, Franklin, Starnes & Holt, PA, Ft Myers, FL; Robert E. Anderson, Jr., Yelsow &

Koeppel, P.A., Fort Myers, FL. Concealed other similar incidents where inmates have died due to delay in care and inadequate care.

KK. WILLIAM WOLFE, Plaintiff, v. IDAHO DEPARTMENT OF CORRECTION; BRENT REINKE; CORIZON MEDICAL SERVICES; RANDY BLADES; DR. WHINNERY; and ALL MEDICAL CARE PROVIDERS CONNECTED TO THE PLAINTIFF'S HEALTH, Defendants. Case No. 1:13-cv-00227-EJL UNITED STATES DISTRICT COURT FOR THE DISTRICT OF IDAHO

Corizon has retained staff who issue whatever declaration/expert report is necessary to defeat claims. Through counsel who have first hand knowledge through information gained through prior litigation For Corizon Medical Services, Defendant: Dylan Alexander Eaton, J Kevin West, LEAD ATTORNEYS, Parson Behle & Latimer, Boise, ID. Concealed evidence that all around the nation Corizon improperly delays medical treatment for diagnosed prostate cancer often causing death. Among other things the cancer would not have spread to lymph nodes had Corizon provided surgery to remove his prostate in a more timely fashion, and also that Corizon improperly delays radiation therapy after the spread of the cancer is.

LL. EDWIN WYLIE-BIGGS, Plaintiff, vs. ORLANDO L. HARPER; WILLIAM EMERICK; JESSE ANDRASCIK; SIMON WAINWRIGHT; LONG Deputy Warden; CORIZON HEALTH SERVICES, Defendants. Civil Action No. 14-1150 UNITED STATES DISTRICT COURT FOR THE WESTERN DISTRICT OF PENNSYLVANIA

Corizon has retained staff who issue whatever declaration/expert report is necessary to defeat claims. Through counsel who have first hand knowledge through information gained through prior litigation For CORIZON HEALTH SERVICES, Defendant: Kathryn M. Kenyon, LEAD ATTORNEY, Meyer, Unkovic & Scott LLP, Pittsburgh, PA. Corizon concealed evidence that it delays treatment and fails to provide pain medication and that there are too many such incidents.

11. Defendant violated 18 U.S.C. 1962(a)(b)(c)(d).

INJURY

12. But for the RICO violation the damages would have been substantial.

SAMPLE RACKETEERING COMPLAINT AGAINST WEXFORD HEALTH SOURCES

United States District Court For the Middle District of Pennsylvania.

PARTIES

1. CHARLES ISELEY, v. WEXFORD HEALTH SERVICES, INC. DOES ONE TO TEN Defendants and each of them are persons capable of holding a legal or beneficial interest in property" 18 U.S.C. 1961(3)

BACKGROUND

2. In CHARLES ISELEY, Appellant v. JEFFREY BEARD; ROBERT BITNER; KENNETH KYLER; FRANK GILLIS; WILMA SEWELL; KANDIS DASCANI; JOSEPH KORT, DIANA BANEY; PATRICIA EVERHART; PATRICIA YARGER; DAWN MILLS, Physician Asst.; PAUL ROEMER; MARY SHOWALTER; KILE; CYNTHIA STEVENS; JOHN SIDLER; PHS, INC.; ASG, INC.; WEXFORD HEALTH SERVICES, INC. No. 02-cv-02006 defendants concealed evidence on issues regarding the denial of HCV treatment, the validity of the DOC HCV protocol, the psychiatric screening requirement, and the consent form requirement.

JURISDICTION AND VENUE

3. WEXFORD transacts its affairs in this district, hence jurisdiction is proper. 18 U.S.C. 1965(a).

ENTERPRISE

4. WEXFORD HEALTH SERVICES, INC., Samuel H. Foreman, Weber, Gallagher, Simpsons, Stapleton, Fires & Newby, Pittsburgh, PA. is the associated in fact enterprise (Weber Gallagher) different and distinct from defendant engaged in and the activities of which affect interstate commerce 18 U.S.C. 1961(4) These fraudulent acts are not isolated but part of a fraudulent pattern of conduct made of hundreds of fraudulent predicate acts, engaged in by defendant, in order to defeat claims and awards.

5. As a direct and proximate cause of defendant's conduct, of the pattern of racketeering activity, plaintiff and other litigants suffered damages to their property.

6. One of the purposes and functions of the enterprise is to engage in the legitimate business of health care and defending lawsuits. The illegitimate business of the enterprise is to perpetrate fraud, conceal evidence, manufacture evidence, defeat valid claims, awards. Defendant knowingly and willfully associated with the enterprise, and conducted and participated in its affairs, directly and/or indirectly, by the predicate acts, acts of racketeering alleged in the complaint violating 18 U.S.C. 1962©. It did so by the use of mails and wires violating 18 U.S.C. 1341, 1331 which is racketeering activity in 18 U.S.C. 1961(1)(B).

7. *Defendant authorized, requested, commanded, ratified, recklessly tolerated the unlawful conduct. It did so as a director, high management agent, acquiring or maintaining an interest in the business and profits of the enterprise, in furtherance of the business and activities of the enterprise.*

8. *Defendant conspired with members of the enterprise to violate 18 U.S.C. 1962(a)(b)(c)*

CONTINUOUS PLUS

9. The following acts show a continuity plus relationship. The RICO statute itself provides that conduct relating to prior litigation may constitute racketeering activity.

REMEDY AND REDEMPTION

PATTERN OF RACKETEERING ACTIVITY

10. Defendants committed at least two acts of racketeering activity one of which occurred after October 15, 1970 and the last act within ten years of the prior act of racketeering through the associated in fact enterprise. They used the United States Mail and wires to engage in this conduct. *These fraudulent acts are not isolated but part of a fraudulent pattern of conduct made of hundreds of fraudulent predicate acts, engaged in by defendant, in order to defeat claims and awards.*

A. CHARLES ISELEY, Appellant v. JEFFREY BEARD; ROBERT BITNER; KENNETH KYLER; FRANK GILLIS; WILMA SEWELL; KANDIS DASCANI; JOSEPH KORT, DIANA BANEY; PATRICIA EVERHART; PATRICIA YARGER; DAWN MILLS, Physician Asst.; PAUL ROEMER; MARY SHOWALTER; KILE; CYNTHIA STEVENS; JOHN SIDLER; PHS, INC.; ASG, INC.; WEXFORD HEALTH SERVICES, INC. No. 02-cv-02006

Defendants concealed evidence as to issues regarding the denial of HCV treatment, the validity of the DOC HCV protocol, the psychiatric screening requirement, and the consent form requirement.

B. STANLEY N. OZOROSKI, Appellant v. DR. FREDERICK R. MAUE, Chief of Clinical Services, Individually and in his official capacity; WEXFORD HEALTH SOURCES, INC.; PRISON HEALTH SERVICES, Individually and in its official capacity; DR. ADAM A. EDELMAN, Individually and in his official capacity; MARVA CERULLO, Health Care Administrator SCI Mahanoy, individually; CECILIA VALASQUEZ, Director of Guadenzia DRC; GAUDENZIA-DRC, All Defendants Jointly and Severally Liable; CHERYL CANTEY, Head Medical Supervisor of Gaudenzia Samuel H. Foreman, Esq., Leah M. Lewis, Esq., Weber, Gallagher, Simpson, Stapleton, Fires & Newby, Pittsburgh, PA.

Defendants conceal the fact that it does not treat inmates and asks prison systems not to provide treatment that is expensive. It also conceals evidence of the fact that it has on staff and retainer doctors and experts who have agreed for a fee to provide whatever testimony Wexford desires to defeat inmate complaints. Acting pursuant to this plan Wexford concealed this Wexford concealed the fact that it has the practice of delaying hernia surgery and that plaintiff would not have been disabled as its expert testified.

C. Galen Lloyd Houser, Plaintiff -vs- Charles L. Ryan, et al., Defendants. CV-13-0200-PHX-GMS (JFM) UNITED STATES DISTRICT COURT FOR THE DISTRICT OF ARIZONA

Wexford has retained staff who issue whatever declaration/expert report is necessary to defeat claims. Through counsel who have first hand knowledge through information gained through prior litigation For Wexford Health Sources Incorporated, ADC Contracted Health Care, Provider for the State of Arizona, (outside the State of Arizona, location not known.), Defendant: Brandi Christine Blair, Edward G Hochuli, LEAD ATTORNEYS, Jones Skelton & Hochuli PLC, Phoenix, AZ. Concealed evidence that Defendant Wexford through the nation has had its contracts cancelled for violating various terms of its contract by failing to provide Plaintiff medical treatment, instituting policies requiring the termination "en masse" of the provision of various medications,

D. Robert Joseph Benge, Plaintiff, v. Charles L. Ryan, et al., Defendants.No. CV 14-0402-PHX-DGC (BSB)UNITED STATES DISTRICT COURT FOR THE DISTRICT OF ARIZONA

Through counsel For Wexford Health Incorporated of Pittsburgh, PA, Defendant: Brandi Christine Blair, Edward G Hochuli, Kenneth Louis Moskow, LEAD ATTORNEYS, Jones Skelton & Hochuli PLC, Phoenix, AZ. Wexford concealed evidence that it is the norm for them to deny treatment for fractures until it is too late, discontinue prescription medications.

REMEDY AND REDEMPTION

E. TOMMY WHITE, SR., Plaintiff-Appellant v. CHRISTOPHER B. EPPS, COMMISSIONER, MISSISSIPPI DEPARTMENT OF CORRECTIONS; RON KING, Superintendent, South Mississippi Correctional Institution-Two; DR. RON WOODALL; NURSE HAM; WEXFORD HEALTH; NURSE APRIL MEGS, Defendants-AppelleesNo. 10-60556 UNITED STATES COURT OF APPEALS FOR THE FIFTH CIRCUIT

Wexford has retained staff who issue whatever declaration/expert report is necessary to defeat claims. Through counsel who have first hand knowledge through information gained through prior litigation. For CHRISTOPHER B EPPS, COMMISSIONER, MISSISSIPPI DEPARTMENT OF CORRECTIONS, RON KING, Superintendent, South Mississippi Correctional Institution-Two, Defendants - Appellees: Charles Baron Irvin, Esq., Office of the Attorney General for the State of Mississippi, Jackson, MS. For RON WOODALL, Doctor, HAM, Nurse, WEXFORD HEALTH, APRIL MEGS, Nurse, Defendants - Appellees: Vardaman Kimball Smith, III, Bryan Nelson, P.A., Hattiesburg, MS. Concealed evidence that inmates have no remedy under PLRA for grievance staff have been directed not to afford relief.

F. TIMOTHY G PRYER, Plaintiff-Appellant v. R. WALKER, Doctor/Health Services Administrator at CMCF III; SHARON PAIGE, Captain, Central MS Correctional Facility III; DR. JOSEPH BLACKSTON; CORRECTIONAL HEALTH SERVICE, INC.; WEXFORD HEALTHCARE RESOURCES; COMMISSIONER CHRISOPHER EPPS; MARGARET BINGHAM, Defendants-AppelleesNo. 08-60867 UNITED STATES COURT OF APPEALS FOR THE FIFTH CIRCUIT

For R WALKER, Doctor/Health Services Administrator at CMCF III, CORRECTIONAL HEALTH SERVICE, Defendants - Appellees: Saundra Brown Strong, Phelps Dunbar, L.L.P., Jackson, MS.For SHARON PAIGE, Captain, Central MS Correctional Facility III, COMMISSIONER CHRISOPHER EPPS, MARGARET BINGHAM, Defendants - Appellees: Charles Baron Irvin, Esq., Pelicia E. Hall, Esq., Special Assistant Attorney General, Office of the Attorney General, for the State of Mississippi, Jackson, MS.For WEXFORD HEALTHCARE RESOURCES, Defendant - Appellee: Joseph A. O'Connell, III, Esq., Vardaman Kimball Smith, III, Bryan Nelson, P.A., Hattiesburg, MS. Wexford has retained staff who issue whatever declaration/expert report is necessary to defeat claims. Through counsel who have first hand knowledge through information gained through prior litigation Concealed evidence that IT IS THE NORM NOT TO PROPERLY DIAGNOSE AND TREAT INMATES CAUSING NUMEROUS DEATHS AND PERMANENT INJURY

G. .JESSICA HANKEY, Individually, and as Administratrix of the Estate of Ryan Rohrbaugh, Appellant v. WEXFORD HEALTH SOURCES, INC.; PRISON HEALTH SERVICES, INC.;
H. MARK BAKER; D.O. ALAN ESPER; DEBORAH O'LEARY, PA-C No. 09-3675 UNITED STATES COURT OF APPEALS FOR THE THIRD CIRCUIT

For JESSICA HANKEY, Individually and as Administratix of the Estate of Ryan Rohrbaugh, Plaintiff - Appellant: Charles W. Marsar, Jr., Esq., Harrisburg, PA.For WEXFORD HEALTH SOURCES, INC., Defendant - Appellee: Patricia L. Dodge, Esq., Joshua R. Lorenz, Esq., Meyer, Unkovic & Scott, Pittsburgh, PA.For O'LEARY, Defendant - Non-Participating: Patricia L. Dodge, Esq., Joshua R. Lorenz, Esq., Meyer, Unkovic & Scott, Pittsburgh, PA.For MARK BAKER, Doctor, Defendant - Appellee: William D. Kennedy, Esq., Rosemary R. Schnall, Esq., White & Williams, Berwyn, PA. Through counsel Wexford concealed they give significant treatment but delay/deny being examined by specialists and that as a direct result the treatment is not effective, causing permanent injury and deaths. Wexford has retained staff who issue whatever declaration/expert report is necessary to defeat claims.

I. KENNETH F. LEONARD, Plaintiff/Appellant, v. FLORIDA DEPARTMENT OF CORRECTIONS, WEXFORD HEALTH SOURCES, INC., DAVID HARRIS, G. SOMODEVILLA, A. PIPIN, J.L. GREEN, AND G.J. SMITH, Defendants/Appellees. 06-11223-FF UNITED STATES COURT OF APPEALS FOR THE ELEVENTH CIRCUIT

REMEDY AND REDEMPTION

Through counsel RITTER CHUSID BIVONA & COHEN, LLP, MITCHEL CHUSID, ESQ., Florida Bar No. 879282, Attorneys for Wexford Health Sources, Inc., Guillermo Somodevilla, and Gail Smith Wexford concealed the fact there are too many instances where it has failed to give medically prescribed supplies causing inmates to suffer. Wexford has retained staff who issue whatever declaration/expert report is necessary to defeat claims.

J. CONTRELL PLUMMER, Plaintiff-Appellant, v. WEXFORD HEALTH SOURCES, INCORPORATED, et al., Defendants-Appellees.No. 14-3314UNITED STATES COURT OF APPEALS FOR THE SEVENTH CIRCUIT

For Wexford Health Sources, Incorporated, MAGID FAHIM, Doctor, Medical Director of Menard, FE FUENTES, Doctor, Defendants - Appellees: Timothy Patrick Dugan, Attorney, Sandberg Phoenix & Von Gontard P.C., St. Louis, MO. Concealed evidence they follow the ineffective course of treatment causing permanent injury and death. Wexford has retained staff who issue whatever declaration/expert report is necessary to defeat claims.

K. RONALD C. MACON, JR., Plaintiff-Appellant, v. SYLVIA MAHONE, DENNIS LARSON, and WEXFORD HEALTH SOURCES, INC., Defendants-Appellees. No. 13-2155 UNITED STATES COURT OF APPEALS FOR THE SEVENTH CIRCUIT

For Sylvia Mahone, Dennis Larson, Wexford Health Sources, Incorporated, Defendants - Appellees (13-2155): Michael John Charysh, Attorney, Charysh & Schroeder, Ltd., Chicago, IL CONCEALED EVIDENCE IINMATES ARE DYING AND PERMANENT INJURY IS CAYSED OFTEN BY THEIR PRACTICE OF DELAYING/DENYING TREATMENT   FOR failing kidneys Wexford has retained staff who issue whatever declaration/expert report is necessary to defeat claims.

L. JUSTIN JAMES HINZO, Plaintiff - Appellant, v. NEW MEXICO CORRECTIONS DEPARTMENT; JOE WILLIAMS; GEORGE TAPIA; WEXFORD HEALTH SOURCES, INC.; CORRECTIONAL MEDICAL SERVICES, INC.; DR. FNU ARNOLD; DR. WILLIAM MIZELL; DR. TONY LNU; DR. DEBRA CLYDE; DR. JOHN STOVER; DR. JOHN DOE (L.C.C.F.); DR. JOHN DOE (C.N.M.C.F.); DR. JOHN DOE (W.N.M.C.F.); DAVID GONZALES, Correctional Officer; WAYNE GALLEGOS; LIANE LOPEZ, R.N.; JERRY ROARK (Deputy Warden); LAWRENCE JARAMILLO, Warden P.N.M.; G.E.O., Defendants - Appellees. No 13-2060UNITED STATES COURT OF APPEALS FOR THE TENTH CIRCUIT

Counsel For WEXFORD MEDICAL SERVICES, Defendant - Appellee: Sebastian A. Dunlap, Edward W. Shepherd, Allen, Shepherd, Lewis & Syra, Albuquerque, NM. For DAVID GONZALES, Defendant - Appellee: Melinda L. Wolinsky, New Mexico Corrections Department, Office of General Counsel, Santa Fe, NM. CONCEALED evidence they deny/delay treatment and has retained staff who issue whatever declaration/expert report is necessary to defeat claims often false.

M. .MANNIE MADDOX, Plaintiff--Appellant, v. WEXFORD HEALTH SOURCES, INC., et al., Defendnts--Appellees.No. 12-1810UNITED STATES COURT OF APPEALS FOR THE SEVENTH CIRCUIT

For WEXFORD HEALTH SOURCES, INCORPORATED, Defendant - Appellee: Brad A. Elward, Attorney, HEYL, ROYSTER, VOELKER & ALLEN, Peoria, IL.For PETER H. KEHOE, Defendant - Appellee: Jack Kiley, Attorney, ERICKSON, DAVIS, MURPHY, JOHNSON, GRIFFITH & WALSH, Decatur, IL.For MARY MILLER, Defendant - Appellee: Carl J. Elitz, Attorney, OFFICE OF THE ATTORNEY GENERAL, Civil Appeals Division, Chicago, IL. Concealed evidence it is the norm to deny/delay treatment for impaired   causing loss very often of the vision. Wexford has retained staff who issue whatever declaration/expert report is necessary to defeat claims.

REMEDY AND REDEMPTION

N. JAMES MATHEW HARRIS, Plaintiff-Appellant, versus CHRISTOPHER B. EPPS, Commissioner, Mississippi Department of Corrections; GLORIA PERRY, Doctor; ROBERT MOORE, Doctor; DAISY THOMAS, Doctor; RONALD WOODALL, Doctor; KEN KAISER, Doctor; JOHN DOE; WEXFORD HEALTH SOURCES, INCORPORATED, Also Known as Wexford Health Services, Defendants-Appellees.No. 12-60701 UNITED STATES COURT OF APPEALS FOR THE FIFTH CIRCUIT

For ROBERT MOORE, Doctor, DAISY THOMAS, Doctor, RONALD WOODALL, Doctor, KEN KAISER, Doctor, WEXFORD HEALTH SOURCES, INCORPORATED, also known as Wexford Health Services, Defendants - Appellees: Vardaman Kimball Smith, III, Bryan Nelson, P.A., Hattiesburg, MS. Concealed evidence they as a matter of practice deny treatment for Hepatitis C infection and back problems. Wexford has retained staff who issue whatever declaration/expert report is necessary to defeat claims.

O. DORCUS WITHERS, Plaintiff-Appellant, v. WEXFORD HEALTH SOURCES, INC., et al., Defendants-Appellees.No. 10-3012 UNITED STATES COURT OF APPEALS FOR THE SEVENTH CIRCUIT

For LOIS MATHES, GERARDO ACEVEDO, Defendants - Appellees: Rachel A. Murphy, Attorney, OFFICE OF THE ATTORNEY GENERAL, Civil Appeals Division, Chicago, IL. For WEXFORD HEALTH SOURCES, INCORPORATED, DEBRA MILLER, R.N., Defendants - Appellees: Brad A. Elward, Attorney, Craig L. Unrath, Attorney, HEYL, ROYSTER, VOELKER & ALLEN, Peoria, IL. Concealed evidence it denies effective treatment for scoliosis, which is lateral curvature of the spine; on an x-ray the spine appears from the front or back to be S- or C-shaped rather than I-shaped. Wexford has retained staff who issue whatever declaration/expert report is necessary to defeat claims.

P. HOYT RAY, Plaintiff-Appellant, v. WEXFORD HEALTH SOURCES, INC., and VIPIN K. SHAH, Defendants-Appellees.No. 12-1774 UNITED STATES COURT OF APPEALS FOR THE SEVENTH CIRCUIT

For WEXFORD HEALTH SOURCES, INCORPORATED, VIPIN K. SHAH, Doctor, Defendants - Appellees: Tamara K. Hackmann, Attorney, HEYL, ROYSTER, VOELKER & ALLEN, Urbana, IL; Matthew Lurkins, Attorney, HEYL, ROYSTER, VOELKER & ALLEN, Springfield, IL; Craig L. Unrath, Attorney, HEYL, ROYSTER, VOELKER & ALLEN, Peoria, IL. . Concealed evidence it denies effective treatment for pain. It examines the patient but does not follow community standards to ensure treatment is effective. Wexford has retained staff who issue whatever declaration/expert report is necessary to defeat claims.

Q. WILLIAM L. LANE, Plaintiff-Appellant, v. WEXFORD HEALTH SOURCES (CONTREATOR); VANESSA SAWYER, Health Care Administrator; PAMILA REDDEN, Defendants-Appellees.No. 11-3552 UNITED STATES COURT OF APPEALS FOR THE SIXTH CIRCUIT

For WEXFORD HEALTH SOURCES (CONTREATOR), PAMILA REDDEN, Defendants - Appellees: Paul-Michael La Fayette, Poling Petrello, Columbus, OH. . Concealed evidence it denies treatment for those disabled with gun shot wounds or discrepancy between the length of his legs. It examines the patient but does not follow community standards to ensure treatment is effective denying special needs to manage such conditions. Wexford has retained staff who issue whatever declaration/expert report is necessary to defeat claims.

R. SOTINA LAVALE CUFFEE, deceased, Estate of, by and through her administrator, Bradley A. Cuffee, Plaintiff - Appellant, v. JOHN R. NEWHART, individually and in his official capacity as Sheriff of the City of Chesapeake, Defendant - Appellee, v. WEXFORD HEALTH SOURCES, INCORPORATED, Third Party Defendant - Appellee.No. 10-1494UNITED STATES COURT OF APPEALS FOR THE FOURTH CIRCUIT

Andrew J. Terrell, Thomas C. Mugavero, WHITEFORD, TAYLOR & PRESTON, LLP, Falls Church, Virginia, for Appellee Wexford Health Sources, Incorporated. . Concealed evidence it denies/delays treatment for those with painful toothache, of severe chest pains, tingling in arms and back, and insomnia frequently causing death. It examines the patient but does not follow community standards to ensure treatment is effective denying special needs to manage such conditions. Wexford has retained staff who issue whatever declaration/expert report is necessary to defeat claims

S. DAVON LYMON, Plaintiff-Appellant, v. ARAMARK CORPORATION; JOSEPH NEUBAUER; CHARLIE CARRIZALES, Defendants, and WEXFORD CORPORATION, JOHN SANCHEZ; ABNER HERNANDEZ; JOE WILLIAMS; NEW MEXICO DEPARTMENT OF CORRECTIONS, Defendants-Appellees. No. 11-2210 UNITED STATES COURT OF APPEALS FOR THE TENTH CIRCUIT

For WEXFORD CORPORATION, Defendant - Appellee: James Roy Wood, Miller Stratvert, Albuquerque, NM. . Concealed evidence it denies/delays treatment for those injured in prison often causing permanent injury.

T. PAUL GRAHAME MORGAN, Plaintiff-Appellant v. STATE OF MISSISSIPPI; ATTORNEY GENERAL OF THE STATE OF MISSISSIPPI; CHRISTOPHER EPPS; E.L. SPARKMAN; RONALD KING; LAWRENCE KELLY; MARGARET BINGHAM; BOBBY KING; DR. BEARRY; RUTHIE HALL, Nurse; MILLIS WASHINGTON; DR. ARNOLD; DR. WALKER; LT. HOLMES; DR. WATTS; DR. MCCLEAVE; DR. RON WOODALL; LIEUTENANT "UNKNOWN" BONNER; CAPTAIN UNKNOWN DAVIS;EMIL DANEFF; WEXFORD HEALTH SOURCES, INC.; JOHN DOE, I, CEO of Correctional Medical Services; JOHN DOE, II, CEO of Wexford Health Sources, Inc.; JASON HOLMES; HUBERT DAVIS; RITA BONNER; CAPTAIN PAGE; CAPTAIN ENLERS; CAPTAIN SIMMS; BRENDA SIMMS; NINA ENLERS; SHARON PAIGE, Defendants-Appellees No. 09-60959 UNITED STATES COURT OF APPEALS FOR THE FIFTH CIRCUIT

For BOBBY KING, JOHN DOE, I, CEO of Correctional Medical Services, ARNOLD, Doctor, RUTHIE HALL, Nurse, Defendants - Appellees: Robert H. Pedersen, Watkins & Eager, P.L.L.C., Jackson, MS.For BEARRY, Doctor, WATTS, Doctor, WALKER, Doctor, Defendants - Appellees: Robert H. Pedersen, Watkins & Eager, P.L.L.C., Jackson, MS; Vardaman Kimball Smith, III, Bryan Nelson, P.A., Hattiesburg, MS.For MILLIS WASHINGTON, MCCLEAVE, Doctor, Defendants - Appellees: Joseph A. O'Connell, III, Esq., Vardaman Kimball Smith, III, Bryan Nelson, P.A., Hattiesburg, MS.For RON WOODALL, WEXFORD HEALTH SOURCES INC, EMIL DANEFF, Defendants - Appellees: Joseph A. O'Connell, III, Esq., Bryan Nelson, P.A., Hattiesburg, MS. Concealed evidence they deny/delay treatment for serious medical needs. They examine the patient but do not follow community standards to ensure treatment is effective. They have retained staff who issue whatever declaration/expert report is necessary to defeat claims

U. JOHN ASHLEY HALE, Plaintiff--Appellant, v. RONALD KING, Superintendent of Southern Mississippi Correctional Institution; MARGARET BINGHAM, Superintendent of Southern Mississippi Correctional Institution; CHRISTOPHER EPPS, Commissioner of Mississippi Department of Corrections; MIKE HATTEN, Health Service Administrator of Wexford for Southern Mississippi Correctional Institution; JOHN DOE, Physician at Southern Mississippi Correctional Institution; DOCTOR ZANDU, Psychiatrist at Central Mississippi Correctional Facility; DOCTOR PATRICK ARNOLD, Physician for Correctional Medical Services at Southern Mississippi Correctional Institution; DOCTOR WILLIAMS, Psychiatrist of Correctional Medical Services for Southern Mississippi Correctional Institution; DOCTOR TRINCA, Physician for Wexford at Southern Mississippi Correctional Institution; MIRIAM MOULDS, Kitchen Supervisor at Southern Mississippi Correctional Institution; JOHN DOE 2, Chief Executive Officer of Correctional Medical Services for Mississippi Department of Corrections; JOHN DOE 3, Chief Executive Officer of Wexford at Southern Mississippi Correctional Institution for Mississippi Department of Corrections; DOCTOR MCCLEAVE; DOCTOR WOODALL; WEXFORD HEALTH SERVICES, Defendants--Appellees. No. 07-60997 UNITED STATES COURT OF APPEALS FOR THE FIFTH CIRCUIT
For PATRICK ARNOLD, Physician for Correctional Medical Services at Southern Mississippi Correctional Institution, Defendant - Appellee: Katie Lofton Wallace, Brunini, Grantham, Grower & Hewes, P.L.L.C.,

Jackson, MS. For TRINCA, Physician for Wexford at Southern Mississippi Correctional Institution, MCCLEAVE, WOODALL, WEXFORD HEALTH SERVICES, Defendants - Appellees: Joseph A. O'Connell, III, Esq., Vardaman Kimball Smith, III, Bryan Nelson, P.A., Hattiesburg, MS. . Concealed evidence they deny/delay treatment for serious medical needs such as chronic Hepatitis C, chronic back problems, and psychiatric conditions They examine the patient but do not follow community standards to ensure treatment is effective. They have retained staff who issue whatever declaration/expert report is necessary to defeat claims

V. OSVALDO C. PALAZON, RONNIE E. CONNOLLY, COLLINS MURRAY, RICARDO PEREZ, WILLIAM BISHOP, WILLIE JONES, AARON KOSBERG, DANIEL MAGLIO, AUSTIN SPEAS, Plaintiffs, KENNETH MCKENNA, Plaintiff-Appellant, versus SECRETARY FOR THE DEPARTMENT OF CORRECTIONS, WEXFORD HEALTH SOURCES INC., DR. HARIDAS NARSI BHADJA, DENISE KELCHNER, Defendants-Appellees, FLORIDA CORRECTIONAL MEDICAL AUTHORITY, Defendant. No. 07-14451 UNITED STATES COURT OF APPEALS FOR THE ELEVENTH CIRCUIT

For Wexford Health Sources Inc., Haridas Bhadja, Dr., Appellees: Mitchel Chusid, Ritter Chusid Bivona & Cohen, LLP, CORAL SPRINGS, FL.For Denise Kelchner, Appellee: Mitchel Chusid, Ritter Chusid Bivona & Cohen, LLP, CORAL SPRINGS, FL; Charles T. Whitelock, Whitelock & Associates, FORT LAUDERDALE, FL. . . Concealed evidence they deny/delay treatment for serious medical needs such as hernia. They examine the patient but do not follow community standards to ensure treatment is effective. They have retained staff who issue whatever declaration/expert report is necessary to defeat claims

W. CHARLES ISELEY, Appellant v. JEFFREY BEARD; ROBERT BITNER; KENNETH KYLER; FRANK GILLIS; WILMA SEWELL; KANDIS DASCANI; JOSEPH KORT, DIANA BANEY; PATRICIA EVERHART; PATRICIA YARGER; DAWN MILLS, Physician Asst.; PAUL ROEMER; MARY SHOWALTER; KILE; CYNTHIA STEVENS; JOHN SIDLER; PHS, INC.; ASG, INC.; WEXFORD HEALTH SERVICES, INC. NO. 06-2465 UNITED STATES COURT OF APPEALS FOR THE THIRD CIRCUIT

For DAWN MILLS, PAUL ROEMER, WEXFORD HEALTH SER, Appellees: Samuel H. Foreman, Weber, Gallagher, Simpsons, Stapleton, Fires & Newby, Pittsburgh, PA. . Concealed evidence they deny/delay treatment for serious medical needs such as including Hepatitis-C ("HCV"), fibromyalgia, chronic fatigue syndrome, and rheumatoid arthritis. They examine the patient but do not follow community standards to ensure treatment is effective. They have retained staff who issue whatever declaration/expert report is necessary to defeat claims

X. SALVATORE CHIMENTI, Appellant v. ROGER KIMBER, Medical Director; BADDICK, Regional Director; ROWE, Wexford Health Sources, Inc.; I. KAUFER, Wexford Health Sources, Inc.; C. POLLOCK, Site Coordinator; FARROHK MOHADJERIN, Former Medical Director; MARTIN F. HORN; ROBERT S. BITNER, Chief Hearing Examiner for the D.O.C.; FREDERICK K. FRANK; PAT YARGER, SCI-Huntingdon Medical Department; P. E. EVERHART, SCI-Huntingdon Medical Department NO. 03-2056 UNITED STATES COURT OF APPEALS FOR THE THIRD CIRCUIT

For PETER BADDICK, Regional Director, ROWE, Wexford Health Sources, Inc., KAUFER, Wexford Health Sources, Inc., POLLOCK, Site Coordinator, FARROHK MOHADJERIN, Dr., Former Medical Director, Appellees: James D. Young, Lavery, Faherty, Young & Patterson, Harrisburg, PA; Patricia L. Dodge, Metz Lewis, Pittsburgh, PA.For MARTIN HORN, ROBERT BITNER, Chief Hearing Examiner for the D.O.C., FREDERICK FRANK, PATRICIA YARGER, SCI-Huntingdon Medical Department, PATRICIA EVERHART, SCI-Huntingdon Medical Department, Appellees: John J. Talaber, Pennsylvania Department of Corrections, Office of Chief Counsel, Camp Hill, PA. Concealed evidence they deny/delay treatment for serious medical needs such as including Hepatitis-C ("HCV"),.. They have retained staff who issue whatever declaration/expert report is necessary to defeat claims

REMEDY AND REDEMPTION

Y. LEONARD T. WILLIAMSON, Appellant v. WEXFORD HEALTH SOURCES, INC.; STATE CORRECTIONAL INSTITUTION, at Pittsburgh (SCIP) Medical Department; DON GEORGE, RN; BONNIE BELL, RN; RACHELLE, RN; NOEL RANKIN, RN; MARSHA HANCOCK, RN; TOM MCDONOUGH, PHYSICIANS ASSISTANT NO. 04-3481 UNITED STATES COURT OF APPEALS FOR THE THIRD CIRCUIT

For WEXFORD HEALTH SER, Appellee: Samuel H. Foreman, Weber, Gallagher, Simpson, Stapleton, Fires & Newby, Pittsburgh, PA. Concealed evidence there are no available remedies under PLRA as grievance staff have been directed not to grant relief They have retained staff who issue whatever declaration/expert report is necessary to defeat claims

Z. 25. RODERIC R. McDOWELL, Plaintiff-Appellant, versus PERNELL BROWN, JOHN DOE, No. 1 WEXFORD HEALTH SOURCES, INC., et al., Defendants-Appellees. No. 04-10272 UNITED STATES COURT OF APPEALS FOR THE ELEVENTH CIRCUIT

For Brown, Pernell, Doe, John, Wexford Health Sources, Inc., ABC Corporation, DEF Corporation, GHA Corporation, JKL Corporation, Appellees: Johnson, Deana Simon, Cruser & Mitchell, LLP, Norcross, GA. Concealed evidence they delay/deny treatment often causing paralysis.

AA. Robert P. Torres, Plaintiff, vs. Charles Ryan, et al., Defendants.No. CV 12-0006-PHX-JAT (DKD)UNITED STATES DISTRICT COURT FOR THE DISTRICT OF ARIZONA

For Charles L Ryan, Named as Charles Ryan, ADOC Director, Defendant: Ashley Brook Zuerlein, LEAD ATTORNEY, Office of the Attorney General - Phoenix, Phoenix, AZ; Michael Evan Gottfried, LEAD ATTORNEY, Office of the Attorney General, Phoenix, AZ. For Dora B Schriro, Former ADOC Director, Robert Jones, M.D., Dennis R Kendall, Medical Programs Director, Defendants: Michael Evan Gottfried, LEAD ATTORNEY, Office of the Attorney General, Phoenix, AZ.For Unknown Lewis, M.D., Unknown Echeverria, M.D., Defendants: Brandi Christine Blair, Edward G Hochuli, LEAD ATTORNEYS, Jones Skelton & Hochuli PLC, Phoenix, AZ. Concealed evidence they deny/delay treatment his Hepatitis C. They have retained staff who issue whatever declaration/expert report is necessary to defeat claims.

BB. Galen Lloyd Houser, Plaintiff -vs- Charles L. Ryan, et al., Defendants.CV-13-0200-PHX-GMS (JFM)UNITED STATES DISTRICT COURT FOR THE DISTRICT OF ARIZONA

Brandi Christine Blair, Edward G Hochuli, LEAD ATTORNEYS, Jones Skelton & Hochuli PLC, Phoenix, AZ. Concealed evidence they deny/delay treatment for migraines, moderate to severe psoriasis, psoriatic arthritis, chronic lower back pain due to disc degeneration, and acid reflux.. They have retained staff who issue whatever declaration/expert report is necessary to defeat claims.

11. Defendant violated 18 U.S.C. 1962(a)(b)(c)(d).

INJURY

12. But for the RICO violation the damages would have been substantial.

REMEDY AND REDEMPTION

APPENDIX A

Barry Northcross Patterson, Plaintiff, vs. Charles L. Ryan, et al., Defendants.

No. CV 05-1159-PHX-RCB

UNITED STATES DISTRICT COURT FOR THE DISTRICT OF ARIZONA

2011 U.S. Dist. LEXIS 95915

August 26, 2011, Decided
August 26, 2011, Filed
SUBSEQUENT HISTORY: Motion granted by, in part, Clarified by, Motion denied by, in part, As moot *Patterson v. Ryan, 2011 U.S. Dist. LEXIS 124753 (D. Ariz., Oct. 25, 2011)*

PRIOR HISTORY: *Patterson v. Ryan, 2010 U.S. Dist. LEXIS 134025 (D. Ariz., Dec. 1, 2010)*

COUNSEL: [*1] Barry Northcross Patterson, Plaintiff, Pro se, FLORENCE, AZ.

For Unknown Moore, Named as Moore, Unknown Broderick, Named as Broderick, K McConnell, Deputy Warden, sued in his/her individual & official capacity, Unknown Soulvie, Named as Soulvie, Unknown Curran, Named as Curran, Defendants: Paul Edward Carter, LEAD ATTORNEY, Office of the Attorney General, Liability Management Section, Tucson, AZ; Sharon S Moyer, LEAD ATTORNEY, Sacks Tierney PA, Scottsdale, AZ.

For Unknown Wilber, Named as Wilber, Defendant: Gregory Dakent Cote, Peter M Coppinger, LEAD ATTORNEYS, McCarter & English LLP, Boston, MA; Sharon S Moyer, LEAD ATTORNEY, Sacks Tierney PA, Scottsdale, AZ.

For K J McConnell, Deputy Warden, Defendant: Paul Edward Carter, Office of the Attorney General, Liability Management Section, Tucson, AZ.

JUDGES: Robert C. Broomfield, Senior United States District Judge.

OPINION BY: Robert C. Broomfield

OPINION

ORDER

After more than six years of litigation, familiarity with which is assumed, a single count remains in plaintiff *pro se* Barry Northcross Patterson's complaint.[1] More specifically, in count I plaintiff asserts claims against defendants Broderick and Mason,[2] both of whom are Arizona Department of Corrections ("ADOC") [*2] chaplains. Allegedly defendants violated plaintiff's free exercise rights under the *First Amendment*, and his rights under the Religious Land Use and Institutionalized Persons Act ("RLUIPA"), *42 U.S.C. § 2000cc et seq.*, by not providing him with a three meal a day kosher diet, despite the fact that he is a Messianic Jew purportedly eligible for a kosher diet under ADOC regulations. Plaintiff is seeking injunctive relief as well as compensatory and punitive damages.

  1 All references to the complaint herein shall be read as referring to the second amended complaint ("SAC") (Doc. 106).
  2 Neither the complaint nor the answer provides the first names of these defendants.

Pending before the court is defendants' motion for partial dismissal. Focusing solely on plaintiff's RLUIPA claim, defendants argue that they are entitled to dismissal of that claim for two reasons. First, defendants argue that the *Eleventh Amendment* bars any RLUIPA claim for damages against them in their official capacities. Second, defendants argue that RLUIPA does not provide a private cause for monetary damages against state officials, like them, in their individual capacities. Alternatively, defendants argue that they are [*3] entitled to qualified immunity from plaintiff's RLUIPA claim for monetary damages. Lastly, regardless of whether plaintiff is asserting his rights under the *First Amendment* or RLUIPA, defendants contend that the court should dismiss as moot his request for an injunction ordering defendants to provide him with a completely kosher diet.

Essentially, plaintiff concedes that the issue of whether RLUIPA allows for the recovery of monetary damages against defendants in either their official or individual capacities is a legal one, properly resolved on this motion. See Supp. Resp. (Doc. 124) at 1 ("Patterson leaves it to this Court or the Supreme Court to decide whether or not he is allowed money damages under RLUIPA."); and at 3 (same). It is difficult to discern exactly what plaintiff's position is regarding the defendants' invocation of qualified immunity. Evidently plaintiff believes that the defendants' reliance upon that doctrine somehow contravenes the Ninth Circuit's instructions on remand. It is clear, however, that plaintiff disagrees that his request for an injunction requiring that he be served three kosher meals daily is moot.

Background

The material facts, taken as true and construed [*4] in the light most favorable to plaintiff as the non-moving party, see *Johnson v. Lucent Technologies Inc., 2011 U.S. App. LEXIS 17520, 2011 WL 3332368, at *8 (9th Cir. 2011)* (citation omitted), are straightforward and few. During his incarceration, plaintiff became a Messianic Jew. SAC (Doc. 106) at 3, ¶ 3. Thereafter, on approximately March 1, 2004, plaintiff filled out an ADOC form requesting a kosher diet, which he claims "is common for many Messianic Judists [sic] who follow many of the Jewish traditions." Id. When he received his first meal pursuant to that request, allegedly it was "not the kosher meal given to Jewish believers[,]" but a "vegetarian meal." Id.

Plaintiff received that vegetarian meal even though he "is not . . . [and] has [n]ever been a vegetarian[.]" Id. According to plaintiff, he was being provided vegetarian breakfasts and lunches, but "standard kosher dinner[s]" because ADOC was informed by a "Jewish Rabbi[] . . . [that] that should suffice for [plaintiff's] religious needs." Id. The thrust of this count is plaintiff's belief that he is being discriminated against because he is a Messianic Jew.

Plaintiff Patterson is currently housed at the Central Arizona Correction Facility ("CACF") [*5] in Florence, Arizona. SAC (Doc. 106) at 1. At the time of the events complained of herein, however, he was housed at an ADOC facility, also in Florence, Arizona. Id. at 1, ¶ 2. Defendants Broderick and Mason maintain that they do not work at that CACF facility, which they describe as a "private prison[.]" Reply (Doc. 125) at 3:24. The SAC is silent, however, as to where defendants are currently working. And because this is a motion to dismiss, the court must confine itself to the allegations in the SAC. The SAC simply alleges that plaintiff encountered those two defendants while at the ADOC facility in Florence, Arizona. SAC (Doc. 106) at 1, ¶ 2; and at 3, ¶ 3.

Discussion

I. Governing Legal Standards

Defendants did not specify which Rule forms the basis for their dismissal motion. However, because defendants are challenging the legal sufficiency of plaintiff's RLUIPA claim, presumably they intended to rely upon *Fed. R. Civ. P. 12(b)(6)*, which allows for dismissal for "failure to state a claim upon which relief can be granted[.]" *Fed. R. Civ. P. 12(b)(6)*. However, because defendants contend that plaintiff's claim for injunctive relief is moot, *Fed. R. Civ. P. 12(b)(1)*, governing motions [*6] to dismiss for lack of subject matter jurisdiction is the proper procedural vehicle for this aspect of defendants' dismissal motion. See *Nasoordeen v. F.D.I.C., 2010 U.S. Dist. LEXIS 32045, 2010 WL 1135888, at *5 (C.D.Cal. 2010)* (citing cases) ("Federal courts lack subject matter jurisdiction to hear claims that are moot.") Regardless of which Rule governs the present motion, plaintiff is entitled to similar safeguards.

"A *Rule 12(b)(6)* motion tests the legal sufficiency of a claim." *Cook v. Brewer, 637 F.3d 1002, 1004 (9th Cir. 2001)*. "A claim may be dismissed only if it appears beyond doubt that the plaintiff can prove no set of facts in support of his claim which would entitle him to relief." Id. (internal quotation marks and citations omitted). "'To survive a motion to dismiss, a complaint must contain sufficient factual matter, accepted as true, to 'state a claim to relief that is plausible on its face.'" *Hinds Investments, L.P. v. Angioli, 654 F.3d 846, 2011 U.S. App. LEXIS 15809, 2011 WL 3250461, at *2 (9th Cir. 2011)* (quoting *Ashcroft v. Iqbal, 556 U.S. 662, 129 S.Ct. 1937, 1949, 173 L.Ed.2d 868 (2009))* (other citation omitted). "Conclusory allegations and unwarranted inferences, however, are insufficient to defeat a motion to dismiss." *Johnson, 2011 U.S. App. LEXIS 17520, 2011 WL 3332368, at *8* [*7] (citation omitted).

"Dismissal is proper where there is either a lack of a cognizable legal theory or the absence of sufficient facts alleged under a cognizable legal claim." *Hinds Investments, 654 F.3d 846, 2011 U.S. App. LEXIS 15809, 2011 WL 3250461, at *2* (citation omitted). At the same time, however, because plaintiff Patterson is proceeding *pro se*, the court "must construe his complaint[] liberally even when evaluating it under the *Iqbal* standard." *Johnson, 2011 U.S. App. LEXIS 17520, 2011 WL 3332368, at *9* (citation omitted).

Likewise, when, as here, defendants are facially attacking subject matter jurisdiction, "factual allegations of the complaint are presumed to be true and conflicts in the pleadings are resolved in the plaintiff's favor." *Kelly v. Public Utility Dist. No. 2, 2011 U.S. Dist. LEXIS 61436, 2011 WL 294166, at *4 (E.D.Wash. 2011)* (citing, inter alia, *Doe v. Holy See,557 F.3d 1066, 1073 (9th Cir.2009)* (internal citations omitted)). With these standards firmly in mind, the court has carefully examined the complaint *vis-a-vis* defendants' motion for partial dismissal.

II. RLUIPA

A. Official Capacity

"The *Eleventh Amendment* bars suits for money damages in federal court against a state, its agencies, and state officials acting in their official capacities." *Aholelei v. Dep't of Pub. Safety, 488 F.3d 1144, 1147 (9th Cir. 2007)* [*8] (citations omitted); see also *Krainski v. Nevada ex rel. Bd. of Regents of NV. System of Higher Educ., 616 F.3d 963, 967 (9th Cir. 2010)* (citation omitted) ("*Eleventh Amendment* immunity . . . shields state officials from official capacity suits.") "The *Eleventh Amendment* bars an action by a private citizen against a state 'unless Congress has abrogated state sovereign immunity under its power to enforce the *Fourteenth Amendment* or [the] state has waived it.'" *Jachetta v. United States, 653 F.3d 898, 2011 U.S. App. LEXIS 15808, 2011 WL 3250450, at *7 (9th Cir. 2011)* (quoting *Holley v. Cal. Dep't of Corr., 599 F.3d 1108, 1111 (9th Cir. 2010)*).

"To abrogate a state's sovereign immunity under § 5 of the *Fourteenth Amendment*, Congress's intent must be 'unequivocally expressed.'" Id. (quoting *Tennessee v. Lane, 541 U.S. 509, 517, 124 S.Ct. 1978, 158 L.Ed.2d 820 (2004)* (internal quotation marks omitted)). "Similarly, a state will be deemed to have waived its immunity 'only where stated by the most express language or by such overwhelming implications from the text as will leave no room for any other reasonable construction.'" Id. (quoting *Edelman v. Jordan, 415 U.S. 651, 673, 94 S.Ct. 1347, 39 L.Ed.2d 662 (1974)* (internal quotation [*9] marks and alteration omitted)); see also *Sossamon v. Texas, U.S. , 131 S.Ct. 1651, 1658, 179 L.Ed.2d 700 (2011)* ("A State's consent to suit must be 'unequivocally expressed' in the text of the relevant statute ... [and] may not be implied." (citations omitted)).

In moving for dismissal of the RLUIPA claim for damages against them in their official capacities as ADOC chaplains, initially defendants solely relied upon *Holley v. Cal. Dep't of Corr., 599 F.3d 1108 (9th Cir. 2010)*. There, the Ninth Circuit, "join[ing] five of the six circuits to have considered th[e] question[,]" held that "RLUIPA's 'appropriate relief' language does not unambiguously encompass monetary damages so as to effect a waiver of sovereign immunity from suit for monetary claims[.]" Id. (internal quotation marks, citation and footnote omitted). Continuing, the Holley Court explained that "[t]he phrase 'appropriate relief' does not address sovereign immunity specifically at all, let alone 'extend [a waiver of sovereign immunity] unambiguously to . . . monetary claims' in particular." Id. (quoting *Lane, 518 U.S., at 192, 116 S.Ct. 2092*). Given that unequivocal holding, Holley supports the view that plaintiff [*10] Patterson has not stated a RLUIPA claim for monetary damages against defendants in their official capacities.

Not only that, the Supreme Court's decision in *Sossamon v. Texas, 131 S. Ct. 1651, 179 L. Ed. 2d 700 (2011)*, which defendants note in a supplemental filing, leaves no doubt that plaintiff Patterson's RLUIPA claim for monetary damages against defendants in their official capacities cannot survive this motion to dismiss. "[G]rounded on the line of *Eleventh Amendment* authority requiring 'clear expression' to abrogate the sovereign immunity of states from damages claims[,]" *Centro Familiar Cristiano Buenas Nuevas v. City of Yuma, 651 F.3d 1163, 2011 U.S. App. LEXIS 14247, 2011 WL 2685288, at *3 (9th Cir. 2011)*, the Sossamon Court held "that States, in accepting federal funding, do not consent to waive their sovereign immunity to private suits for money damages under RLUIPA because no statute expressly and unequivocally includes such a waiver. *Sossamon, 131 S.Ct. at 1663, 179 L.Ed.2d 700*. Therefore, this court finds that the *Eleventh Amendment* bars plaintiff Patterson's RLUIPA claim insofar as he is seeking monetary damages from defendants Broderick and Mason in their official capacities. As such, defendants are entitled to dismissal [*11] of that claim.

B. Individual Capacity

Construing the complaint as alleging a RLUIPA claim for damages against them in their individual capacities,[3] defendants argue that the court should dismiss that claim because it is not cognizable. The Ninth Circuit has not yet "ruled . . . in a precedential opinion[]"[4] on the issue of whether RLUIPA "appli[es] to private actors sued for damages in their individual capacity." *Florer, 639 F.3d at 922 n. 3*. Indeed, as recently as April 15, 2011, the Ninth Circuit has continued to "reserve" on that "question for another day." Id. Likewise, the Supreme Court has not yet decided whether persons can be sued in their individual capacities for damages under RLUIPA.[5] Nonetheless, given the weight of soundly reasoned authority set forth herein, the court agrees with defendants and dismisses plaintiff's RLUIPA claims against them for monetary damages in their individual capacities.

> 3   It is beyond peradventure that *pro se* complaints must be "liberally construed[.]" *Florer v. Congregation Pidyon Shevuyim, N.A., 639 F.3d 916, 923 n. 4 (9th Cir. 2011)*. So, even though plaintiff Patterson's complaint does not explicitly allege that defendants are being sued both in [*12] their official and individual capacities, that is a reasonable inference based upon a liberal construction of the complaint. Thus, as did the defendants, this court is treating plaintiff's claims against defendants Broderick and Mason as being brought against them in both capacities.
>
> 4   As the Fifth Circuit observed in Sossamon, "[t]he Ninth Circuit appears to have assumed that a cause of action for monetary relief against state actors in their individual capacities exists, but its cases contain no analysis and are unpublished." *Sossamon, 560 F.3d at 327 n. 23* (citing *Campbell v. Alameida, 295 Fed.Appx. 130, 131 (9th Cir. 2008)* (mem.) (unpublished); *Von Staich v. Hamlet, Nos. 04-16011 & 06-17026, ___ Fed.Appx. ___, ___, 2007 U.S. App. LEXIS 24528, 2007 WL 3001726, at *2 (9th Cir. Oct. 16, 2007)* (mem.) (unpublished)); see also *Shilling v. Crawford, 377 Fed.Appx. 702, 705 (9th Cir. 2010)* (declining to "settle th[e] question" of "whether money damages for RLUIPA claims are available against state actors sued in their individual capacities because even assuming *arguendo* that such damages would otherwise be available, the defendants in this case are entitled to qualified immunity[]").
>
> 5   The Supreme Court's grant of certiorari [*13] in Sossamon was limited to the following question: "Whether an individual may sue a State or state official in his official capacity for damages for violations of the Religious Land Use and Institutionalized Persons Act, *42 U.S.C. § 2000cc et seq. (2000 ed.)*." *Sossamon v. Texas, 130 S.Ct. 3319, 176 L.Ed.2d 1218 (2010)*. Necessarily then, the Supreme Court did not address the Fifth Circuit's further holding in Sossamon there is no cause of action under RLUIPA for individual capacity claims.

As the Ninth Circuit has acknowledged, "[t]he Fifth, Seventh, and Eleventh Circuits have held that RLUIPA does not provide an action for damages for individual-capacity claims." *Florer, 639 F.3d at 922 n. 3* citing *Sossamon v. Lone Star State of Tex., 560 F.3d 316, 327-28 & n. 23 (5th Cir. 2009); Nelson v. Miller, 570 F.3d 868, 889 (7th Cir. 2009); Smith v. Allen, 502 F.3d 1255, 1272-75 (11th Cir. 2007))*; see also *Rendelman v. Rouse, 569 F.3d 182, 184 (4th Cir. 2009)* (holding that "when invoked as a spending clause statute, RLUIPA does not authorize a claim for money damage against an official sued in her individual capacity[]"). Consequently, even in the absence of Ninth Circuit case law squarely addressing [*14] the issue, numerous district courts within this Circuit likewise have declared that RLUIPA does not provide for damages claims against officials sued in their individual capacities. See, e.g., *Florer v. Bales-Johnson*, 752 F. Supp. 2d 1185, 1205-1206 (W.D.Wash. 2010) (footnote omitted) (dismissing claim regarding, *inter alia,* kosher meals because "individual Defendants cannot be held liable in their individual capacities in an action under RLUIPA[]"); *Parks v. Brooks*, 2010 U.S. Dist. LEXIS 138135, 2010 WL 5186071, *1-*2 (D.Nev. 2010); *Sokolsky v. Voss*, 2010 U.S. Dist. LEXIS 75892, 2010 WL 2991522, *2-*4 (E.D.Cal. 2010); *Alvarez v. Hill*, 2010 U.S. Dist. LEXIS 12637, 2010 WL 582217, *11 (D.Or. 2010); *Harris v. Schriro*, 652 F.Supp.2d 1024, 1030 (D.Ariz. 2009).

There is no reason here for the court to depart from this weight of soundly reasoned authority. Particularly persuasive is the Spending Clause analysis of the Fifth, Seventh and Eleventh Circuits. Following that reasoning, in *Harris v. Schriro*, 652 F.Supp.2d 1024 (D.Ariz. 2009), the court cogently wrote:

> RLUIPA creates a cause of action for suits against 'a government'; government is defined as '(i) a State county, municipality, or other governmental entity created under the authority of a State; (ii) a branch, department, [*15] agency, instrumentality, or official of an entity listed in [that] clause . . .; and (iii) any other person acting under color of state law . . . .' 42 U.S.C. § 2000cc-5. As the court in *Sossamon* noted, this language appears to create a right against state actors in their individual capacities and it even mirrors the 'under color of' language in § 1983. 560 F.3d at 327-28. But the Fifth, Seventh and Eleventh Circuits nevertheless held that individuals may not be sued for damages under RLUIPA. The Eleventh Circuit reasoned that RLUIPA was enacted pursuant to Congress's Spending Clause power, not pursuant to the *Section 5 power of the Fourteenth Amendment,* citing *Cutter v. Wilkinson,* 544 U.S. 709, 715-16, 125 S.Ct. 2113, 161 L.Ed.2d 1020 (2005), and that Spending Clause legislation is not legislation in its operation but operates like a contract, *see Pennhurst State Sch. & Hosp. v. Halderman,* 451 U.S. 1, 17, 101 S.Ct. 1531, 67 L.Ed.2d 694 (1981). *Smith,* 502 F.3d at 1273-75. Individual RLUIPA defendants are not parties to the contract in their individual capacities, and therefore, only the grant recipient-that is, the state-may be liable for its violation. *Id.*
>
> The Fifth Circuit also concluded [*16] that RLUIPA was passed pursuant to the Spending Clause and noted that it also followed the same rule for Spending Clause legislation. *Sossamon,* 560 F.3d at 328-29. Likewise, the Seventh Circuit reasoned that '[c]onstruing RLUIPA to provide for damages actions against officials in their individual capacities would raise serious questions regarding whether Congress had exceeded its authority under the Spending Clause,' and so the court declined to read RLUIPA as allowing damages against defendants in their individual capacities. *Nelson,* 570 F.3d at 889.

That *Id.* at 1029-1030. Spending Clause analysis is particularly apropos given that the Ninth Circuit has "upheld RLUIPA as a constitutional exercise of Congress' spending power." *San Jose Christian College v. City of Morgan Hill,* 360 F.3d 1024, 1034 (9th Cir. 2004) (citation omitted).

Moreover, although noting RLUIPA's "ostensibl[e] . . . *Commerce Clause* underpinnings[,]" in Nelson the Seventh Circuit "interpret[ed] RLUIPA as an exercise of Congress's power under the Spending Clause[]" where there was "no evidence . . . that plaintiff's denial of a religious diet affect[ed] . . . commerce with foreign nations, among the several States, [*17] or with Indian tribes." *Nelson,* 570 F.3d at 886 (internal quotation marks and citation omitted) (citing *Smith,* 502 F.3d at 1274 n. 9 (reasoning that RLUIPA should be analyzed as an exercise of Congress's Spending Clause authority when there is no evidence of an effect on interstate or international commerce); *Sossamon,* 560 F.3d at 328 n. 34 (same)).

Similarly, here, plaintiff Patterson's allegations that he has been denied a three meal a day kosher diet do not appear to implicate the *Commerce Clause.* See *Mahone v. Pierce County,* 2011 U.S. Dist. LEXIS 62617, 2011 WL 3298898, at *5 (W.D.Wash. May 23, 2011), adopted in full by 2011 U.S. Dist. LEXIS 62617, 2011 WL 3298528 (W.D.Wash. Aug. 1, 2011)(treating RLUIPA as an exercise of Congress's Spending Clause power where there was "no evidence of an effect on interstate or international commerce by an alleged denial of ["Jewish Kosher Meals three times a day"] to indicate that RLUIPA should be interpreted under the *Commerce Clause*[]"); *Sokolsky v. Voss,* 2010 U.S. Dist. LEXIS 75892, 2010 WL 2991522, at *4 n. 4 ("Plaintiff's allegations that he was denied a proper Kosher . . . for Passover diet do not appear to implicate the *Commerce Clause*."); *Harris*, 652 F.Supp.2d at 1030 (citation omitted) (Jewish inmate's claim, *inter alia*, that [*18] prison refused to modify his kosher diet meals did "not appear to implicate the *Commerce Clause* and so the Court interpret[ed] RLUIPA as a Spending Clause enactment[]"). Thus, following the rationale first set forth by the Eleventh Circuit in *Smith*, and subsequently adopted by the Fourth, Fifth and Seventh Circuits, the court holds that plaintiff Patterson cannot obtain monetary relief against defendants Broderick and Mason in their individual capacities for allegedly violating RLUIPA. Accordingly, the court grants defendants' motion to dismiss in that regard.

III. Qualified Immunity

Having found that the complaint fails to state a RLUIPA claim for damages against defendants in either their official or individual capacities, there is no need to consider defendants' alternative argument that they are entitled to qualified immunity on such claim. See *Sokolsky*, 2010 U.S. Dist. LEXIS 75892, 2010 WL 2991522, at *4 ("[B]ecause this court finds that RLUIPA creates no right to recovery for damages against state officials acting in their individual capacities, the Court declines to reach" the qualified immunity "question.") (citing *Sossamon*, 560 F.3d at 327 ("Of course, if no private right of action exists against the defendants [*19] in their individual capacities, then a qualified immunity ... analysis would be unnecessary."); see also *Alvarez*, 2010 U.S. Dist. LEXIS 12637, 2010 WL 582217, at *11 (citing Sossamon in support of the court's decision to decline to reach a qualified immunity analysis once it found that individual damages were not available against defendants)). If the court were to consider this argument, though, it would grant defendants' request for qualified immunity primarily because it was not until nearly four years after the events complained of herein that the Ninth Circuit interpreted RLUIPA with respect to the provision of kosher meals. See *Shakur v. Schriro*, 514 F.3d 878 (9th Cir. 2008). Thus, it is entirely plausible that defendants Broderick and Mason had no notice of the evolving status of the law in this Circuit on this question until *after* the conduct complained of herein.

IV. Injunctive Relief

In addition to seeking monetary damages, plaintiff is seeking "[a] Court Order requiring 3 [three] Kosher meals or the equivalent for all Kosher diets[.]" SAC (Doc. 106) at 13, ¶ E. Defendants offer several reasons for dismissing as moot this claim for injunctive relief. There is no need to address each of those reasons, however, [*20] because one is dispositive; that is, plaintiff Patterson "is receiving *precisely* the diet that he is seeking by way of injunctive relief in this action." See Reply (Doc. 124) at 4:11 (emphasis added).

As defendants stress, and plaintiff concedes, he has been "given his main request - 3 kosher meals[.]" Resp. (Doc. 124) at 4. Indeed, plaintiff acknowledges that he was granted that request "about 6 months after he filed this case[,]" *i.e.*, roughly six months after April 15, 2005, or, more than six years ago. See id. Not only that, presumably based upon the foregoing, in April, 2010, plaintiff sought an order, *inter alia*, "enjoining the ADC from *discontinuing* the 3-meal-a-day kosher diet that he currently receives," and "'*moot*[ing] his action as complete[.]'" *Patterson v. Schriro*, 2010 U.S. Dist. LEXIS 100187, 2010 WL 3522500, at *1 (D.Ariz. 2010) (emphasis added) (citing Mot. (Doc. 87)).[6] In denying that preliminary injunction motion, this court explained that plaintiff did not "set forth any facts indicating that he [wa]s subject to a threat of irreparable harm" where he did "not explain why an order to *maintain* his kosher diet [wa]s necessary nor d[id] he present any facts showing that his current kosher diet is [*21] likely to be discontinued or changed in the future." 2010 U.S. Dist. LEXIS 100187, [WL] at *2 (emphasis added). As to plaintiff's request to moot the action, the court found that because it had recently granted plaintiff leave to amend his complaint, that "indicate[d] his desire to proceed with this litigation[.]" Id. (citation omitted).

6   The court takes judicial notice of plaintiff's earlier motion and the court's decision relating thereto, as well as plaintiff's response to the pending motion. See *Spectravest, Inc. v. Mervyn's Inc.*, 673 F.Supp. 1486, 1490 (N.D.Cal. 1987) (citation omitted) ("Court may take judicial notice of the existence of an earlier pleading, particularly when the same parties are involved.") The court may take judicial notice in its discretion even absent a specific request for judicial notice ("RJN") by a party. See *Rodriguez v. SGLC, Inc.*, 2010 U.S. Dist. LEXIS 74466, 2010 WL 2943128, at *1 n. 4 (E.D.Cal. 2010) (granting defendants' RJNs, although such requests where "unnecessary for pleadings in ths same case[]"). By taking judicial notice,

there is no need, as defendants suggest, to convert this aspect of their dismissal motion to one for summary judgment. See Mot. (Doc. 115) at 10:20, n. 4.

Given that plaintiff is [*22] receiving the kosher diet that he is seeking through an injunction, defendants argue that this claim is moot because no case or controversy exists as Article III requires. Plaintiff disagrees, arguing that "ADOC & CACF regularly take his diet for false reasons and an injunction might prevent him from such abuse." Supp. Resp. (Doc. 124) at 1. Defendants retort that the issue of whether those "previous suspensions and delays . . . were justified is not . . . before the Court." Reply (Doc. 125) at 4:9-10. Even if they were, defendants reiterate that an injunction requiring plaintiff to receive a "'complete daily' kosher diet (when available)[,]" nonetheless is moot due to the lack of a case or controversy. See Resp. (Doc. 116) at 2.

Article III of the Constitution limits the jurisdiction of the federal courts to "Cases" or "Controversies." See *U.S. Const. art. III, § 2, cl. 1.* "The doctrine of mootness, which is embedded in Article III's case or controversy requirement, requires that an actual, ongoing controversy exist at all stages of federal court proceedings." *Pitts v. Terrible Herbst, Inc., 653 F.3d 1081, 2011 U.S. App. LEXIS 16368, 2011 WL 3449473, at *3 (9th Cir. 2011)* (citing *Burke v. Barnes, 479 U.S. 361, 363, 107 S.Ct. 734, 93 L.Ed.2d 732 (1987)).* [*23] "Whether 'the dispute between the parties was very much alive when suit was filed . . . cannot substitute for the actual case or controversy that an exercise of this [c]ourt's jurisdiction requires.'" Id. (quoting *Honig v. Doe, 484 U.S. 305, 317, 108 S.Ct. 592, 98 L.Ed.2d 686 (1988)).* "A case becomes moot 'when the issues presented are no longer 'live' or the parties lack a legally cognizable interest in the outcome' of the litigation." Id. (quoting *Powell v. McCormack, 395 U.S. 486, 496, 89 S.Ct. 1944, 23 L.Ed.2d 491 (1969)).* "In other words, if events subsequent to the filing of the case resolve the parties' dispute," the court "*must* dismiss the case as moot" because the court does "not have the constitutional authority to decide moot cases[.]" Id. (internal quotation marks and citations omitted) (emphasis added).

Applying those well-settled rules to the present case, it is patently obvious that plaintiff Patterson's request for "[a] court order requiring 3 kosher meals or the equivalent for all kosher diets, no vegetarian[,]" SAC (Doc. 106 at 6, ¶ E(1), is moot. Since shortly after the filing of this lawsuit, plaintiff Patterson has been receiving the very kosher diet for which he [*24] requests injunctive relief. Hence, there is no longer any "present controversy as to which [that] relief can be granted." See *Johnson v. Rancho Santiago Cmty. Coll. Dist., 623 F.3d 1011, 1018 (9th Cir. 2010)* (citation omitted), cert. denied, *131 S. Ct. 2096, 179 L. Ed. 2d 891 (U.S. 2011).* Consequently, the court GRANTS defendants' motion to dismiss for lack of subject matter jurisdiction insofar as plaintiff is seeking injunctive relief requiring that he be provided three kosher meals. That particular claim is moot.

Because the court finds that none of these three claims can be cured by allegations of other facts, defendants' motion herein is granted with prejudice. See *Balsam v. Tucows Inc., 627 F.3d 1158, 1163 n. 3 (9th Cir. 2010)* (citation omitted) ("because no amendment could cure the defect in [plaintiff's] claims[,] [t]he district court did not err in dismissing the complaint with prejudice[]").

For the foregoing reasons, IT IS ORDERED that:

(1) the reference to the Magistrate Judge is WITHDRAWN as to defendants' "Amended Motion to Dismiss RLUIPA and Injunction Claims" (Doc. 115);

(2) Defendants' "Amended Motion to Dismiss RLUIPA and Injunction Claims" (Doc. 115) is GRANTED with [*25] prejudice.

REMEDY AND REDEMPTION

Barry Northcross Patterson, Plaintiff, vs. Charles L. Ryan, et al., Defendants.

No. CV 05-1159-PHX-RCB (SPL)

UNITED STATES DISTRICT COURT FOR THE DISTRICT OF ARIZONA

2012 U.S. Dist. LEXIS 75289

May 30, 2012, Decided
May 31, 2012, Filed

SUBSEQUENT HISTORY: Affirmed by *Patterson v. Moore*, 2015 U.S. App. LEXIS 1749 (9th Cir. Ariz., Feb. 3, 2015)

PRIOR HISTORY: *Patterson v. Ryan*, 2011 U.S. Dist. LEXIS 149516 (D. Ariz., Dec. 29, 2011)

COUNSEL: [*1] Barry Northcross Patterson, Plaintiff, Pro se, FLORENCE, AZ.

For Unknown Moore, Named as Moore, Unknown Soulvie, Named as Soulvie, Unknown Broderick, Named as Broderick, Defendants: Paul Edward Carter, LEAD ATTORNEY, Office of the Attorney General, Liability Management Section, Tucson, AZ; Sharon S Moyer, LEAD ATTORNEY, Sacks Tierney PA, Scottsdale, AZ.

For Unknown Wilber, Named as Wilber, Defendant: Gregory Dakent Cote, LEAD ATTORNEY, McCarter & English LLP, Boston, MA; Sharon S Moyer, LEAD ATTORNEY, Sacks Tierney PA, Scottsdale, AZ.

For K J McConnell, Deputy Warden, Defendant: Paul Edward Carter, Office of the Attorney General, Liability Management Section, Tucson, AZ.

For Unknown Mason, Named as Mason - Chaplain, sued in his/her individual & official capacity, Defendant: Paul Edward Carter, LEAD ATTORNEY, Office of the Attorney General, Liability Management Section, Tucson, AZ.

JUDGES: Robert C. Broomfield, Senior United States District Judge.

OPINION BY: Robert C. Broomfield

OPINION

ORDER

Plaintiff Barry Northcross Patterson brought this civil rights action pursuant to *42 U.S.C. § 1983* against Arizona Department of Corrections (ADC) Chaplains G. Broderick and Wayne F. Mason (Doc. 106). Before the Court is Defendants' [*2] Motion for Summary Judgment (Doc. 145), which Plaintiff opposes (Doc. 150).

The Court will grant summary judgment to Defendants but deny their request for attorney's fees.

I. Background

Plaintiff initiated this action in April 2005 and filed a First Amended Complaint in May 2005 (Docs. 1, 7). The case proceeded on three counts against seven ADC Defendants; Plaintiff's claims concerned the alleged denial of a religious diet and a retaliatory transfer (Doc. 10). In January 2007, the Court granted Defendants' motions to dismiss and for summary judgment and entered judgment in favor of Defendants and against Plaintiff (Docs. 71-72). Plaintiff appealed, and the Ninth Circuit Court of Appeals affirmed in part and vacated in part and remanded Plaintiff's *First Amendment* religious-diet claim against Broderick and Mason in light of the intervening decision in *Shakur v. Schriro, 514 F.3d 878, 885-88 (9th Cir. 2008)* (Doc. 81). Plaintiff was permitted to file a Second Amended Complaint to add a claim under the Religious Land Use and Institutionalized Persons Act (RLUIPA), *42 U.S.C. § 2000cc et seq.* (Docs. 100, 106). Plaintiff's RLUIPA claim was subsequently dismissed by the Court (Doc. 127).

The sole [*3] remaining claim in Plaintiff's Second Amended Complaint is his allegation that Defendants violated his *First Amendment* free-exercise rights when they denied him kosher breakfasts and lunches even though he is a Messianic Jew eligible for a kosher diet under ADC regulations (Doc. 106 at 3). Plaintiff averred that he received vegetarian breakfasts and lunches and only his dinners were kosher (id. at 3-3A). He requested compensatory and punitive damages (id. at 6). [1]

> 1   The Court granted Defendants' Motion to Dismiss for lack of subject matter jurisdiction as to Plaintiff's request for injunctive relief because he has received three kosher meals a day since late-2005; thus, his claim for injunctive relief was moot (Doc. 127 at 14-17).

Defendants now move for summary judgment on the grounds that (1) they are not liable because they merely responded to Plaintiff's administrative complaints, (2) Plaintiff's desire to keep kosher is not sincerely held or rooted in religious belief, (3) there were legitimate penological reasons for serving Plaintiff a diet with just one kosher meal a day; and (4) they are entitled to qualified immunity (Doc. 145).

II. Summary Judgment Standard

A court must grant [*4] summary judgment "if the movant shows that there is no genuine dispute as to any material fact and the movant is entitled to judgment as a matter of law." *Fed. R. Civ. P. 56(a)*; see also *Celotex Corp. v. Catrett, 477 U.S. 317, 322-23, 106 S. Ct. 2548, 91 L. Ed. 2d 265 (1986)*. Under summary judgment practice, the movant bears the initial responsibility of presenting the basis for its motion and identifying those portions of the record, together with affidavits, that it believes demonstrate the absence of a genuine issue of material fact. *Celotex, 477 U.S. at 323*.

If the movant meets its initial responsibility, the burden then shifts to the nonmovant to demonstrate the existence of a factual dispute and that the fact in contention is material, i.e., a fact that might affect the outcome of the suit under the governing law, and that the dispute is genuine, i.e., the evidence is such that a reasonable jury could return a verdict for the nonmovant. *Anderson v. Liberty Lobby, Inc., 477 U.S. 242, 248, 250, 106 S. Ct. 2505, 91 L. Ed. 2d 202 (1986)*; see *Triton Energy Corp. v. Square D. Co., 68 F.3d 1216, 1221 (9th Cir. 1995)*. The nonmovant need not establish a material issue of fact conclusively in its favor; it is sufficient that "the claimed factual dispute be [*5] shown to require a jury or judge to resolve the parties' differing versions of the truth at trial." *First Nat'l Bank of Ariz. v. Cities Serv. Co., 391 U.S. 253, 288-89, 88 S. Ct. 1575, 20 L. Ed. 2d 569 (1968)*.

At summary judgment, the judge's function is not to weigh the evidence and determine the truth but to determine whether there is a genuine issue for trial. *Anderson, 477 U.S. at 249*. In its analysis, the court must believe the nonmovant's evidence, and draw all inferences in the nonmovant's favor. *Id. at 255*.

III. Facts

With their summary judgment briefing, the parties each submit a separate Statement of Facts and supporting exhibits, including declarations, grievance documents, Plaintiff's deposition, and copies of ADC policies (Doc. 146, Defs.' Statement of Facts (DSOF); Doc. 151, Pl.'s SOF (PSOF)). Many of the parties' factual assertions are not relevant for the reasons set forth in the analysis. The relevant undisputed and disputed facts underlying Plaintiff's claim are as follows:

Plaintiff is a Messianic Jew, and in 2004, when he was housed at the Rynning Unit, he requested a kosher diet (PSOF ¶ 1). Broderick informed Plaintiff that he was approved for the "Kosher Diet Plan" as of March 10, 2004, and as soon [*6] as Plaintiff received his "diet card" he would begin receiving the Kosher diet (DSOF ¶ 31; PSOF ¶ 31). But instead of a full kosher diet, Plaintiff was provided with a vegetarian breakfast and lunch and a kosher dinner (DSOF ¶ 2; PSOF ¶ 2). Plaintiff never requested a vegetarian diet, and at the time he requested a kosher diet and was approved for it, he was unaware that the "Kosher Diet Plan" did not consist of three kosher meals a day (PSOF ¶¶ 2, 32).

Defendants state that before 2005, ADC offered two kosher-diet plans, identified in the Food Service System policy as the "Regular Kosher" diet plan and the "Orthodox Kosher" diet plan; the "Orthodox Kosher" diet plan was only for inmates who were Orthodox Jews (DSOF ¶ 60, Ex. E, Attach. 4, 912-T-OP §§ 912.10, 1.5.2-1.5.3). The Restricted Diet Order form, used to formally request a special diet, does not provide for two kosher meal plans; the only option is the "Kosher Diet Plan," which Plaintiff requested (PSOF ¶ 60, Ex. 5).

In late March 2004, Plaintiff submitted two inmate letters complaining that he was not receiving a kosher diet (DSOF ¶ 32; PSOF ¶ 32). In his April 2, 2004 response, Broderick advised Plaintiff that his approved [*7] Kosher Diet Plan consisted of one kosher meal and two ovo-lacto vegetarian meals, unlike the Orthodox Kosher Diet that consisted of three kosher meals (id.). On April 16, 2004, Plaintiff submitted another inmate letter to Broderick on this issue; Senior Chaplain Sabbagh responded and informed Plaintiff that ADC Central Office had established and approved different kosher diets for Orthodox and non-Orthodox Jewish inmates (DSOF ¶ 33; PSOF ¶ 33).

Plaintiff was subsequently transferred to the Florence-South Unit where Mason was assigned (DSOF ¶ 37). In June 2004, Plaintiff informed Mason that he did not want the vegetarian/kosher combination diet, and he requested the kosher diet plan (DSOF ¶ 45(b); PSOF ¶ 45(b)). In July 2004, Plaintiff submitted a grievance seeking three kosher meals a day (DSOF ¶ 45(e); PSOF ¶ 45(e)).

On July 1, 2005, ADC switched from the two kosher meal plans to one meal plan for all inmates receiving a kosher diet (DSOF ¶ 60).

IV. Parties' Arguments

A. Defendants' Motion

Defendants first argue that they cannot be liable for violating Plaintiff's constitutional rights because they merely responded to Plaintiff's administrative complaints and inquiries, and Mason once [*8] explained the kosher-diet history to Plaintiff (Doc. 145 at 3-4). According to Defendants, Plaintiff did not qualify for the full kosher diet, which they refer to as the Ashelman diet, because he was not an Orthodox Jew (id. at 4).[2] Defendants contend that because they lacked authority to change ADC policy that limited full kosher diets to Orthodox inmates, they are entitled to judgment (id.).

2   This name refers to the Stipulated Final Judgment from Ashelman v. Wawrzaszek, CV 83-1072-PHX (MS), which required ADC to provide Orthodox Jewish inmates with certified kosher meals.

Next, Defendants argue that Plaintiff's desire to keep kosher is not sincerely held or rooted in religious belief as evidenced by conduct that is inconsistent with his claim to keep kosher (id. at 4-5). They state that Plaintiff was a recent convert to Messianic Judaism who showed a willingness to violate kosher rules and little familiarity with his professed faith (id. at 5).

Defendants submit that if the Court finds that Plaintiff did have a sincere religious belief to keep kosher and that their conduct implicated Plaintiff's *First Amendment* rights, they are still entitled to summary judgment because ADC had legitimate [*9] penological reasons to serve Plaintiff the combination diet (id. at 5-6). Defendants argue that ADC had a security interest in streamlining their food service and an interest in preserving scarce financial resources by providing food services within their budgetary constraints and without wasting money with costly meals for inmates who do not partake of them (id. at 6-7). In support, Defendants point to the increase in kosher diet requests and costs since ADC changed its policy in 2005 to provide completely kosher diets to non-Orthodox inmates (id. at 7). Defendants also argue that Plaintiff had alterative means of exercising his right to religious practice, and they assert that Plaintiff could still eat fruits, vegetables, eggs, and dairy products to supplement his combination meal plan (id. at 8).

Defendants contend that granting Plaintiff's special diet request would have effectively given him "carte blanche to make ADC provide [him] with a complete, kosher-certified diet on request" (id.). They again point to the results of the 2005 diet change and argue that there was a significant impact on prison resources and staff as the cost for kosher diets became prohibitive (id. at 8-9).

Lastly, [*10] Defendants assert that even if their conduct was found to have implicated Plaintiff's constitutional rights, they are entitled to qualified immunity (id. at 9). They state that they were administering the ADC policy that provided for a combination kosher meal plan, that this meal plan had been approved by a rabbinical authority, and that no reasonable official in their position would have known that this policy and meal plan violated Plaintiff's *First Amendment* rights (id. at 11). Defendants seek summary judgment and an award of attorneys' fees under *42 U.S.C. § 1988* (id.).

B. Plaintiff's Response[3]

> 3   The Court issued a Notice, required under *Rand v. Rowland, 154 F.3d 952, 962 (9th Cir. 1998)*, that informed Plaintiff of the requirements of *Federal Rule of Civil Procedure 56* and *Local Rule of Civil Procedure 56.1* (Doc. 147).

Plaintiff opposes Defendants' motion (Doc. 150). He asserts that he requested a kosher diet, and the ADC diet request form only listed one kosher meal plan; thus, there was no indication that he would receive a vegetarian-kosher combination diet (id. at 1). Plaintiff states that he "was not, is not, nor wants to be a vegetarian" (id.). Plaintiff asserts that Defendants [*11] approved a kosher diet for him and then intentionally provided something different without any regard for Plaintiff's religious beliefs (id. at 2).

Plaintiff notes the inconsistency between Defendants' authority to approve a religious diet for him and their claim now that they were not authorized to allow Plaintiff to receive a religious diet meeting his needs (id. at 2). Plaintiff suggests that they simply do not want "to accept the responsibility for the constant religious abuse directed against [him]" (id. at 5). Plaintiff also contends that Defendants' argument that they could not provide Plaintiff a full kosher diet for financial reasons is belied by the fact that they have provided full kosher diets to all Orthodox and non-Orthodox Jewish inmates for the last eight years (id. at 1-2). Plaintiff claims that he was denied the requested religious diet because Defendants had a "single-minded purpose" to keep Plaintiff from eating kosher (id. at 4).

Plaintiff maintains that contrary to Defendants' assertions, he has never conceded that keeping kosher is not a central tenet of his faith, and he avers that his request for a kosher diet is based on a sincere religious belief (id. at 4, 6). [*12] He states that he tries to follow God's word and accepts the kosher meals he is allowed and, when he is refused a kosher meal, he eats what he knows is kosher and tries to sustain himself, or he simply stops eating altogether (id. at 5). Plaintiff further states that just because he may eat kosher items from another inmate's tray or from the commissary, it does not mean that his desire to eat kosher is not sincere (id. at 6).

Plaintiff argues that Defendants' current claim that he was denied a full kosher diet because he was not an Orthodox Jew is a new claim and it is not the real reason for the denial in 2004 (id.). He alleges that Defendants lied to him, refused the approved diet, tried to force him to be a vegetarian, and have "continued to abuse him for 8 years with lies, retribution & illegal religious tickets and punishments" (id.).

C. Defendants' Reply

Defendants note that Plaintiff acknowledges that the kosher/vegetarian diet he was provided conformed to his conception of kosher, given his assertion that it is the nature of the food rather than its preparation that is important (Doc. 155 at 4-5). Defendants assert that a vegetarian diet, by definition, cannot contain meat products [*13] forbidden by kosher laws; thus, the vegetarian/kosher diet served Plaintiff's purposes and did not implicate his *First Amendment* rights (id. at 5).

Defendants argue that to the extent Plaintiff challenges the 2004 ADC policy that allowed for two different kosher meal plans, they did not enact that policy; they were just involved in its administration (id. at 4-5). Thus, Defendants reiterate that they cannot be liable for a constitutional violation (id.). They also reiterate their arguments that Plaintiff's desire to keep kosher was not sincerely held, that there were legitimate penological reasons to serve Plaintiff the combination diet, and that they are entitled to qualified immunity (id. at 5-8).

V. Governing Legal Standard

"Inmates retain the protections afforded by the *First Amendment*, 'including its directive that no law shall prohibit the free exercise of religion.'" *Shakur, 514 F.3d at 883-84* (quoting *O'Lone v. Estate of Shabazz, 482 U.S. 342, 348, 107 S. Ct. 2400, 96 L. Ed. 2d 282 (1987)).* To implicate the *Free Exercise Clause*, a prisoner must show that the belief at issue is both "sincerely held" and "rooted in religious belief." *Malik v. Brown, 16 F.3d 330, 333 (9th Cir. 1994);* see *Shakur, 514 F.3d at 884-85*   [*14] (noting the Supreme Court's disapproval of the centrality test and finding that the sincerity test in Malik determines whether the *Free Exercise clause* applies).

Once that showing is made, an inmate must establish that prison officials substantially burden the practice of his religion by preventing him from engaging in conduct which he sincerely believes is consistent with his faith. *Shakur, 514 F.3d at 884-85.*

Finally, even if a prison regulation burdens an inmate's free exercise of religion, the regulation is valid if is reasonably related to legitimate penological interest. *Turner v. Safley, 482 U.S. 78, 89, 107 S. Ct. 2254, 96 L. Ed. 2d 64 (1987).* "Lawful incarceration brings about the necessary withdrawal or limitation of many privileges and rights, a retraction justified by the considerations underlying our penal system." *Shakur, 514 F.3d at 884* (quoting *O'Lone, 482 U.S. at 348*). To determine if a regulation is valid, courts must consider four factors: (1) whether there is a rational connection between the regulation and the asserted government interest; (2) whether there are alternative means of exercising the right; (3) whether accommodation of the right will impact the prison or other inmates; and (4) whether   [*15] there is an absence of ready alternatives. *Turner, 482 U.S. at 89-90.*

VI. Analysis

A. Liability

Before conducting an analysis under the *First Amendment*, the Court addresses Defendants' argument that they should be dismissed because they "merely responded" to Plaintiff's complaints and inquiries (Doc. 145 at 3-4). Defendants' unsuccessfully raised this same argument in their first summary judgment motion (Doc. 47 at 8). For the same reasons as set forth in its prior Order, the Court will not dismiss Defendants on this basis (Doc. 71 at 8).

B. Sincerely Held Belief

Defendants present the exact same argument they submitted in their first summary judgment motion, and rely on the same pre-Malik case law, to assert that Plaintiff's desire to keep kosher was not sincerely held or rooted in religious belief (compare Doc. 47 at 10 with Doc. 145 at 4-5). See *Malik, 16 F.3d at 333* (establishing the sincerity test to determine whether *Free Exercise Clause* applies). Again, Defendants' argument fails. Despite evidence of religious conversions or occasional behavior contrary to purported religious views, Plaintiff professes a belief in Messianic Judaism and the need to abide by kosher dietary laws (see   [*16] Doc. 150 at 4, 6; Doc. 151, PSOF ¶¶ 1, 8, 11-12, 70, 87-88). On Defendants' motion, all facts and the inferences therefrom must be construed in Plaintiff's favor. *Anderson, 477 U.S. at 255.* For the Court to determine that Plaintiff's beliefs are not sincere, it would have to find that Plaintiff is not credible, which it cannot do on summary judgment. See id. Defendants' request for summary judgment on this ground will be denied.

C. Burden on Religious Practice

As mentioned, the protections of the *Free Exercise Clause* are triggered when prison officials substantially burden the practice of an inmate's religion by preventing him from engaging in conduct which he sincerely believes is consistent with his faith. *Shakur, 514 F.3d at 884-85.* With respect to accommodation of various religious affiliations, prison authorities are not responsible for duplicating every religious benefit provided to other religions so that all religions are treated exactly the same. See *Cruz v. Beto, 405 U.S. 319, 322, n. 2, 92 S. Ct. 1079, 31 L. Ed. 2d 263 (1972)* ("[w]e do not suggest . . . that every religious sect or group within a prison--however few in number--must have identical facilities or personnel. A special chapel or place of worship

[*17] need not be provided for every faith regardless of size; nor must a chaplain, priest, or minister be provided without regard to the extent of the demand"); see also *Allen v. Toombs, 827 F.2d 563, 568-69 (9th Cir. 1987)* (prison administrators need not provide each inmate with the spiritual counselor of his or her choice). Thus, the fact that Plaintiff--a Messianic Jew--was denied the exact same kosher diet plan provided to Orthodox Jewish inmates, by itself, does not violate Plaintiff's free-exercise rights.

Instead, Plaintiff must show that the combination vegetarian/kosher meal plan that he was provided burdened his practice of religion. Unlike the prisoner-plaintiff in Shakur, Plaintiff does not allege that the vegetarian diet provided by the prison caused him gastrointestinal problems or any other health problems that in turn substantially burdened his religious activities. See *514 F.3d at 885* (given the plaintiff's sincere belief in consuming kosher meat and the gastrointestinal distress caused by the vegetarian diet, which interfered with his religious activities, the prison's refusal to provide a kosher meat diet implicated the *Free Exercise Clause*).

Nor does Plaintiff allege that [*18] the vegetarian/kosher combination diet did not adhere to his religious beliefs. Plaintiff states that pursuant to his beliefs, all vegetables are kosher, and he "gladly eats grains, fruits, vegetables, eggs, milk & dairy products without complaint" because "its all kosher" (Doc. 151, PSOF ¶ 26; Doc. 150 at 7). See *Ashelman v. Wawrzaszek, 111 F.3d 674, 675 n. 2 (9th Cir. 1997)* (fruits and vegetables and some cereals are kosher). As Defendants point out, Plaintiff's conception of kosher is based on the nature of the food and not its preparation (Doc. 155 at 4-5). Indeed, as Plaintiff states in his response, he believes that he can accept a regular food tray and eat only the kosher items or exchange the non-kosher meat for other kosher items and still satisfy his beliefs (Doc. 150 at 4). He also states that his religious beliefs are not burdened by the denial of any specific food, such as pie or turkey (Doc. 146, DSOF ¶ 20; Doc. 151, PSOF ¶ 20).

In short, Plaintiff provides no specific facts or evidence, or even an allegation, that the vegetarian/kosher diet interfered with or burdened his religious practice. Instead, Plaintiff establishes that he is not a vegetarian and he did not like [*19] being forced to consume a vegetarian diet to keep kosher (see Doc. 151, PSOF ¶ 26). Plaintiff's allegations and evidence also demonstrate that Defendants provided a misleading diet request form and were not entirely forthright when they approved him for a kosher diet but did not inform him that it was actually a combination vegetarian/kosher diet. But none of this implicates the *First Amendment* where there is no showing that Plaintiff's religious practice was burdened as a result. See *Shakur, 514 F.3d at 884-85*.

Plaintiff's allegations that Defendants wrongfully issued him tickets for "sharing" food, that they abused him with "lies" and "retribution," or that they otherwise retaliated against him are beyond the scope of this action, which relates solely to whether the provision of a vegetarian/kosher diet rather than a full kosher diet violated Plaintiff's *First Amendment* free-exercise rights (see Doc. 150 at 6). The Court finds that there is no genuine dispute of material fact whether Plaintiff's religious practice was burdened by the vegetarian/kosher diet. Accordingly, the *First Amendment* is not implicated, and Defendants are entitled to summary judgment. See *Shakur, 514 F.3d at 884-85*.

In [*20] light of this determination, the Court need not conduct an analysis under Turner to determine whether the ADC's 2004 two kosher meal plan served a legitimate penological interest, nor is it necessary to address Defendants' qualified immunity argument.

VII. *42 U.S.C. § 1988*

Under *§ 1988*, a district court may award attorney's fees to a prevailing defendant only if the plaintiff's underlying claim is frivolous or without foundation. *Maag v. Wessler, 993 F.2d 718, 719 (9th Cir. 1993)*. The Court does not find that Plaintiff's claims were frivolous or without foundation; therefore, it will deny Defendants' request for attorney's fees.

IT IS ORDERED:

(1) The reference to the Magistrate Judge is withdrawn as to Defendants' Motion for Summary Judgment (Doc. 145).

(2) Defendants' Motion for Summary Judgment (Doc. 145) is granted in part and denied in part as follows:
    (a) the motion is granted as to summary judgment in favor of Defendants on the remaining *First Amendment* claim;

APPENDIX B

STANLEY N. OZOROSKI, Appellant v. DR. FREDERICK R. MAUE, Chief of Clinical Services, Individually and in his official capacity; WEXFORD HEALTH SOURCES, INC.; PRISON HEALTH SERVICES, Individually and in its official capacity; DR. ADAM A. EDELMAN, Individually and in his official capacity; MARVA CERULLO, Health Care Administrator SCI Mahanoy, individually; CECILIA VALASQUEZ, Director of Guadenzia DRC; GAUDENZIA-DRC, All Defendants Jointly and Severally Liable; CHERYL CANTEY, Head Medical Supervisor of Gaudenzia DRC

No. 11-2042

UNITED STATES COURT OF APPEALS FOR THE THIRD CIRCUIT

460 Fed. Appx. 94; 2012 U.S. App. LEXIS 153

December 12, 2011, Submitted Under Third Circuit LAR 34.1(a)
January 4, 2012, FiledNOTICE: NOT PRECEDENTIAL OPINION UNDER THIRD CIRCUIT INTERNAL OPERATING PROCEDURE RULE 5.7. SUCH OPINIONS ARE NOT REGARDED AS PRECEDENTS WHICH BIND THE COURT.

PLEASE REFER TO *FEDERAL RULES OF APPELLATE PROCEDURE RULE 32.1* GOVERNING THE CITATION TO UNPUBLISHED OPINIONS.

PRIOR HISTORY: [**1]
On Appeal from the United States District Court for the Middle District of Pennsylvania. (D.C. No. 1-08-cv-00082). District Judge: Honorable Christopher C. Conner.
Ozoroski v. Maue, 2011 U.S. Dist. LEXIS 34588 (M.D. Pa., Mar. 31, 2011)

COUNSEL: For STANLEY N. OZOROSKI, Plaintiff - Appellant: Robin J. Gray, Esq., Reading, PA.

For FREDERICK MAUE, Chief of Clinical Services, Individually and in his Official capacity, MARVA CERULLO, Health Care Administrator SCI Mahanoy, individually, Defendants - Appellees: Laura J. Neal, Esq., Pennsylvania Department of Corrections, Office of Chief Counsel, Mechanicsburg, PA.

For WEXFORD HEALTH SOURCES INC, Defendant - Appellee: Samuel H. Foreman, Esq., Leah M. Lewis, Esq., Weber, Gallagher, Simpson, Stapleton, Fires & Newby, Pittsburgh, PA.

For PRISON HEALTH SERVICES, Individually and in its official capacity, ADAM A. EDELMAN, Individually and in his official capacity, Defendants - Appellees: Alan S. Gold, Esq., Gold & Ferrante, Jenkintown, PA.

For CICILIA VALASQUEZ, Director of Guadenzia DRC, CHERYL CANTEY, Head Medical Supervisor of Gaudenzia DRC, Defendants - Appellees: Thomas E. Brenner, Esq., Goldberg & Katzman, Harrisburg, PA.

For GAUDENZIA-DRC, All Defendants Jointly and Severally Liable, Defendant - Non-Participating: Thomas E. [**2] Brenner, Esq., Goldberg & Katzman, Harrisburg, PA.

JUDGES: Before: SLOVITER, VANASKIE, Circuit Judges and STENGEL,[*] District Judge.
   [*] Hon. Lawrence F. Stengel, United States District Court for the Eastern District of Pennsylvania, sitting by designation.

OPINION BY: SLOVITER

OPINION

[*96] SLOVITER, *Circuit Judge.*

Stanley Ozoroski appeals from the District Court's grant of summary judgment against him on his claims that the Appellees denied him access to necessary medical treatment in violation of his *Eighth Amendment* rights.[1]

> 1   The District Court had jurisdiction under *28 U.S.C. §§ 1331* and *1343(a)(3)* and *(4)*. We have jurisdiction under *28 U.S.C. § 1291*. We exercise plenary review of the District Court's grant of summary judgment, and we apply the same standard applicable in the District Court found in *Fed. R. Civ. P. 56. See Doe v. C.A.R.S. Prot. Plus, Inc., 527 F.3d 358, 362 (3d Cir. 2008).*

I.

Because we write primarily for the parties, our recitation of the facts and procedural history is brief. Ozoroski, an inmate in the Pennsylvania state correctional system, suffered a small bowel perforation[2] during a hernia repair operation in 1993. As a result, Ozoroski underwent multiple corrective surgeries shortly thereafter. [**3] Despite ongoing treatment, however, Ozoroski continued to experience abdominal problems and developed an enterocutaneous fistula.[3]

> 2   A small bowel perforation is an abnormal opening in the proximal portion of the intestine distal to the stomach. *See* STEDMAN'S MEDICAL DICTIONARY 247, 1456 (28th ed. 2006).
> 3   An enterocutaneous fistula is an abnormal passage connecting the intestine and skin of the abdomen. STEDMAN'S MEDICAL DICTIONARY 735-36 (28th ed. 2006).

Although Ozoroski requested additional surgery to address his abdominal issues, the Pennsylvania Department of Corrections ("DOC") ultimately chose to pursue a non-surgical course of treatment. In fact, while in DOC custody, Ozoroski was treated and evaluated by more than 20 physicians. While some physicians recommended surgery as a potential way to repair Ozoroski's abdomen, others believed that the risks of surgery ultimately outweighed any potential benefits.[4] The DOC therefore denied Ozoroski's repeated requests for surgery. Nevertheless, approximately 13 years after his initial hernia operation, Ozoroski was released into the custody of Gaudenzia Drug Rehabilitation Center[5] ("Gaudenzia") and, during his stay, he underwent surgery [**4] to repair his abdomen.

> 4   As one physician stated, a surgical correction of Ozoroski's condition would involve "the possibility of severe lifetime disability, debility and even death." App. at 151.
> 5   Although Ozoroski was transferred to the Gaudenzia Drug Rehabilitation Center, he remained under the control of the DOC.

Subsequently, Ozoroski filed a complaint in federal court under *42 U.S.C. § 1983*, alleging that the prison health services and individual medical personnel deprived him of necessary medical treatment during his incarceration at the state correctional institutions at SCI-Rockview and SCI-Mahanoy respectively, and during his subsequent stay at Gaudenzia. After several defendants were dismissed by the District Court, the Court granted summary judgment for the remaining Defendants. Ozoroski timely appealed.

II.

Ozoroski claims that the District Court erred by finding that Dr. Frederick [*97] Maue, Chief of Clinical Services of the Bureau of the Department of Corrections; Marva Cerullo, a healthcare administrator at SCI-Mahanoy; and Wexford Health Sources, Inc., a corporation that previously contracted with the DOC to provide healthcare services to inmates, were entitled to summary judgment [**5] under the applicable statute of limitations because of the Continuing Violations Doctrine. We disagree.

"The statute of limitations period for a *§ 1983* claim arising in Pennsylvania is two years." *Kach v. Hose, 589 F.3d 626, 634 (3d Cir. 2009)*. That period begins to run "when the plaintiff knows or has reason to know of the injury which is the basis of the *section 1983* action." *Genty v. Resolution Trust Corp., 937 F.2d 899, 919 (3d Cir. 1991)*. The Continuing Violations Doctrine, however, is an "equitable exception to the timely filing requirement," which applies "when a defendant's conduct is part of a continuing practice" and is "more than the occurrence of isolated or sporadic acts." *Cowell v. Palmer Twp., 263 F.3d 286, 292 (3d Cir. 2001)*. Under the Doctrine, "an action is timely so long as the last act evidencing the continuing practice falls within the limitations period." *Id.*

Here, Ozoroski's claims against Wexford, Dr. Maue and Cerullo do not fall within the Continuing Violations exception. In particular, Wexford contracted with the DOC to provide healthcare services to inmates from September 1996 to August 31, 2003. Ozoroski, however, did not file the underlying action until January [**6] 14, 2008 - more than four years later. Thus, even under the most expansive interpretation of the Continuing Violations Doctrine, it would not apply to the claims against Wexford, since the corporation had no authority to provide Ozoroski with medical care during the two-year limitations period.

Further, the Doctrine does not extend to Ozoroski's claims against Dr. Maue or Cerullo because their alleged conduct was not connected to any "continuing practice" but instead amounted to isolated incidents. In fact, Dr. Maue's involvement in Ozoroski's treatment was limited to two letters dated November 10, 2003 and October 20, 2004, which stated that it was his medical opinion and that of other physicians that surgery was not in Ozoroski's best interests. As the District Court appropriately reasoned, "[t]he two letters amount to little more than discrete, isolated events not appropriately linked to some larger scheme to deny Ozoroski's medical care." App. at 10. Ozoroski's claims against Cerullo rest on an equally isolated event - her refusal to permit an application for pre-release to be filed on Ozoroski's behalf. Furthermore, since Ozoroski filed a grievance in connection with Cerullo's [**7] refusal to file his pre-release application on November 9, 2004, we find that her conduct was sufficiently permanent to "trigger [Ozoroski's] awareness of and duty to assert his . . . rights" during the limitations period. *Cowell, 263 F.3d at 292*. Nevertheless, he did not bring suit until more than three years after Cerullo and Dr. Maue's alleged conduct. Therefore, his claims against Cerullo and Dr. Maue are also barred as untimely.

Ozoroski also argues that the District Court erred by granting summary judgment on his *Eighth Amendment* claims in favor of Prison Health Services, Inc. ("PHS"), another healthcare provider contracted to provide healthcare services to DOC inmates; Dr. Adam Edelman, director of PHS; Cecilia Velasquez, director of Gaudenzia; and Cheryl Cantey, head medical supervisor of Gaudenzia.

To establish *Eighth Amendment* liability against a private employer, such as PHS, the prisoner must "provide evidence that [*98] there was a relevant PHS policy or custom . . . that . . . caused the constitutional violation [he] allege[s]." *Natale v. Camden Cnty. Corr. Facility, 318 F.3d 575, 584 (3d Cir. 2003)*. The District Court did not err in finding that Ozoroski presented insufficient [**8] evidence to establish an *Eighth Amendment* violation. As the District Court noted, his treating and consulting physicians had varying views on whether surgery was appropriate to treat his condition. The record demonstrates that Dr. Edelman exercised his professional judgment and we can find no evidence that he consciously disregarded Ozoroski's medical needs. Moreover, Ozoroski failed to show that Velasqez or Cantey demonstrated deliberate indifference to his serious medical needs once he reached Gaudenzia, where he continued to attend various medical appointments and ultimately obtained surgery to repair his abdomen.

Ozoroski contends that PHS maintained a policy and practice "of focusing on medical costs instead of the patient's best interest." Appellant's Br. at 28. In support of his claims, he offers a peer review article, an online newspaper article noting that Wexford terminated its contract due to soaring costs, and a 2008 PHS white paper discussing the rising costs of providing healthcare services.[6] These documents contain only general information regarding the delivery of cost-effective healthcare and therefore fail to create a material question as to whether PHS maintained [**9] a policy or custom that caused the deprivation of Ozoroski's constitutional rights.[7]

6   With regard to his claims against Wexford, Appellant also submitted copies of Wexford's website pages, which discuss Wexford's goal of providing cost-effective healthcare to its clients. Although we decide Appellant's claims against Wexford on statute of limitations grounds, we note that Appellant's evi-

dence also fails to establish that Wexford maintained a policy or custom that caused the deprivation of Appellant's constitutional rights.

7   The parties dispute whether these documents constitute inadmissible hearsay evidence. *See Smith v. City of Allentown, 589 F.3d 684, 693 (3d Cir. 2009)* ("Hearsay statements that would be inadmissible at trial may not be considered for purposes of summary judgment."). Even assuming *arguendo* that the documents are admissible, they do not provide a basis for imposing Section 1983 liability.

III.

For the foregoing reasons, we will affirm the District Court's entry of summary judgment in all respects.

APPENDIX C

John Kristoffer Larsgard, Plaintiff, vs. Corizon Health, Inc., Defendant.

No. CV 13-01747-PHX-SPL (JFM)

UNITED STATES DISTRICT COURT FOR THE DISTRICT OF ARIZONA

2014 U.S. Dist. LEXIS 150333

October 21, 2014, Decided
October 21, 2014, Filed

COUNSEL: [*1] For John Kristoffer Larsgard, individually, Plaintiff: Nemer Hadous, LEAD ATTORNEY, Price Law Group APC, Tempe, AZ.

For Corizon Health Incorporated, a Delaware Corporation, Defendant: Heather Alexander Neal, Joseph Scott Conlon, William W Drury, Jr., LEAD ATTORNEYS, Renaud Cook Drury Mesaros PA, Phoenix, AZ.

JUDGES: Honorable Steven P. Logan, United States District Judge.

OPINION BY: Steven P. Logan

OPINION

WO

ORDER

Plaintiff John Kristoffer Larsgard, through counsel, brought this civil rights Complaint under *42 U.S.C. § 1983* against Defendant Corizon Health Incorporated (Corizon), a private corporation contracted to provide medical services for the Arizona Department of Corrections (ADC) (Doc. 1). Before the Court is Corizon's Motion for Summary Judgment (Doc. 32).

The Court will deny the motion and direct Corizon to file a new summary judgment motion.

I. Background

In his Complaint, Larsgard set forth two counts for relief: a medical-care claim under the *Eighth Amendment* (Count I) and a gross negligence/negligence claim under state law (Count II) (Doc. 1 ¶¶ 36-56). Larsgard alleged that when he entered the ADC in April 2012, he had a pre-existing spinal condition that caused chronic, severe pain, muscle spasms, and seizures (*id.* ¶ 14). He claimed that [*2] in December 2012, he suffered a seizure, fell out of bed, and injured his neck and spine (*id.* ¶¶ 14-15). The fall caused further nerve damage and left him partially paralyzed, and shortly thereafter, he underwent emergency surgery on his neck and spine (*id.* ¶¶ 15-17, 19). According to Larsgard, following surgery, the treating neurosurgeon, Dr. Ali A. Baaj, recommended that Larsgard see a pain-management specialist for his chronic, severe pain and receive follow-up treatment within 30 days, including MRI/CT scans, so that a neurologist could evaluate whether his spine was properly healing and the bolts in his neck and spine remained in place (*id.* ¶ 20). Larsgard alleged that despite these recommendations, he was not returned for follow up until late July 2013, six months later, and at that time, the x-rays and MRI imagings had not yet been taken (*id.* ¶ 21).

Larsgard averred that as of the date of his Complaint (August 23, 2013), he had not seen a pain management specialist for his chronic, severe pain (*id.* ¶ 22). He further averred that his medication is ineffective and inadequate to control his seizures, muscle spasms, and neuropathic pain, and the medication that is provided is routinely [*3] out of supply or discontinued for non-medical reasons (*id.*).

Larsgard seeks injunctive and declaratory relief for the alleged *Eighth Amendment* violation ((*id.* ¶¶ 40-46). Specifically, he requests an injunction against Corizon to (1) perform the requisite imaging studies of his neck and spine; (2) refer him to a pain management specialist; and (3) timely administer his medications (Doc. 39 at 2). Larsgard also seeks compensatory and punitive damages and costs (Doc. 1 ¶¶ 57-60).

Corizon moves for summary judgment only on the *Eighth Amendment* claim (*see* Doc. 32). It argues that (1) there is no evidence it denied adequate medical care or had the culpable state of mind required for deliberate indifference and (2) Larsgard merely presents a difference of opinion regarding treatment (Doc. 32).

In his opposition, Larsgard concedes that Corizon has performed the requisite imagings; therefore, that particular request for injunctive relief is moot (Doc. 39 at 2).

II. Summary Judgment Standard

A court must grant summary judgment "if the movant shows that there is no genuine dispute as to any material fact and the movant is entitled to judgment as a matter of law." *Fed. R. Civ. P. 56(a)*; *see also Celotex Corp. v. Catrett, 477 U.S. 317, 322-23, 106 S. Ct. 2548, 91 L. Ed. 2d 265 (1986)*. The movant bears the initial responsibility of presenting [*4] the basis for its motion and identifying those portions of the record, together with affidavits, that it believes demonstrate the absence of a genuine issue of material fact. *Celotex, 477 U.S. at 323*.

If the movant fails to carry its initial burden of production, the nonmovant need not produce anything. *Nissan Fire & Marine Ins. Co., Ltd. v. Fritz Co., Inc., 210 F.3d 1099, 1102-03 (9th Cir. 2000)*. But if the movant meets its initial responsibility, the burden shifts to the nonmovant to demonstrate the existence of a factual dispute and that the fact in contention is material, i.e., a fact that might affect the outcome of the suit under the governing law, and that the dispute is genuine, i.e., the evidence is such that a reasonable jury could return a verdict for the nonmovant. *Anderson v. Liberty Lobby, Inc., 477 U.S. 242, 248, 250, 106 S. Ct. 2505, 91 L. Ed. 2d 202 (1986)*; *see Triton Energy Corp. v. Square D. Co., 68 F.3d 1216, 1221 (9th Cir. 1995)*. The nonmovant need not establish a material issue of fact conclusively in its favor, *First Nat'l Bank of Ariz. v. Cities Serv. Co., 391 U.S. 253, 288-89, 88 S. Ct. 1575, 20 L. Ed. 2d 569 (1968)*; however, it must "come forward with specific facts showing that there is a genuine issue for trial." *Matsushita Elec. Indus. Co., Ltd. v. Zenith Radio Corp., 475 U.S. 574, 587, 106 S. Ct. 1348, 89 L. Ed. 2d 538 (1986)* (internal citation omitted); *see Fed. R. Civ. P. 56(c)(1)*.

At summary judgment, the judge's function is not to weigh the evidence and determine the truth but to determine whether there is a genuine issue for trial. *Anderson, 477 U.S. at 249*. In its analysis, the court must believe the nonmovant's evidence and draw all inferences in the nonmovant's favor. *Id. at 255*. The court need consider [*5] only the cited materials, but it may consider any other materials in the record. *Fed. R. Civ. P. 56(c)(3)*. Where the plaintiff seeks injunctive relief, the court may also consider developments that postdate the motions to determine whether an injunction is warranted. *Farmer v. Brennan, 511 U.S. 825, 846, 114 S. Ct. 1970, 128 L. Ed. 2d 811 (1994)*.

III. Relevant Disputed and Undisputed Facts

In 2009, Larsgard underwent posterior cervical fusion surgery in Germany (Doc. 33, Def.'s Statement of Facts (DSOF) ¶ 2); Doc. 40, Pl.'s Controverting Statement of Facts (PCSF) ¶ 2). In December 2012, while in ADC custody, Larsgard fainted in his cell and hit the back of his head, which caused upper extremity paresthesia and neck pain (DSOF ¶ 3; PCSF ¶ 3). This pain was exacerbated on January 1, 2013, when Larsgard turned his head and lost consciousness (*id.*). He was taken to the emergency room and later admitted to the University of Arizona Medical Center, where x-rays revealed a C6 fracture (Doc. 40, Pl.'s Statement of Facts (PSOF) ¶ 1 & Ex. 1 (Doc. 40-1 at 5)[1]).[2] Larsgard underwent a posterior cervical fusion and laminectomy performed by Dr. Ali Baaj (DSOF ¶ 3; PCSF ¶ 3). Thereafter, on January 11, 2013, Larsgard was transferred to a rehabilitation facility, and Dr. Baaj prescribed a list of medications, [*6] which included narcotics and benzodiazepines (DSOF ¶ 4; PCSF ¶ 4).[3] Upon

Larsgard's discharge, Dr. Baaj recommended he return for follow up 3 weeks after surgery, and a typical follow up is usually 2-3 weeks after surgery, then again at 3 months, and then at 6 months (PCSF ¶ 8).[4]

> 1 Additional citation refers to the document and page number in the Court's Case Management/Electronic Case Filing system.
> 2 Corizon objects to parts of PSOF ¶ 1 and some of the Exhibits cited in support of PSOF ¶ 1; however, there are no objections to the assertion that Larsgard suffered a fractured cervical spine or to Exhibit 1 (Doc. 42 at 1).
> 3 The list of prescribed medications included the following: Tramadol, Salsalate, Phenytoin, Nortriptyline, Neurontin (also known as Gabapentin), Clonazepam, Citalopram, Senna, Bisacodyle, Docusate, morphine tablets and Dilaudid tablets for pain, and Robaxin and Soma for muscle spasms (DSOF ¶ 4; PCSF ¶ 4).
> 4 Corizon objects to PCSF ¶ 8 on the grounds that PCSF ¶ 8 does not really dispute DSOF ¶ 8, it is actually a separate statement of fact, it contains improper arguments, and it does not include citation to the record for some arguments (Doc. 42 ¶ 5). The objection is overruled. [*7] PCSF ¶ 8 disputes an impression presented in DSOF ¶ 8 regarding Larsgard's follow up, and the asserted facts are supported by the cited medical record (see Doc. 40, Ex. 9 at 9, 11-12 (Doc. 40-9 at 9-12)).

Larsgard received pain management treatment post-surgery at the Medical Center and the rehabilitation facility; however, the parties dispute whether this pain management treatment was with a specialist (PSOF ¶ 2; Doc. 42 ¶ 2). Dr. Baaj has recommended pain management treatment since the surgery (PSOF ¶ 2; Doc. 42 at 2).

On February 11, 2013, after Larsgard's return to prison, prison physician Dr. Kevin Lewis noted that in addition to the MS Contin (morphine) prescribed by Dr. Baaj for post-surgical pain, Larsgard had a history of taking a high dose of opioids from 2009 (DSOF ¶ 6; PCSF ¶ 6). Prior to his incarceration, Larsgard was treated by a physician in Norway for chronic, severe neck pain (PSOF ¶ 3).[5] The Norwegian physician tried alternative treatments and pain medications but determined that a combination of opioids and benzodiazepines was the only effective treatment for Larsgard's severe pain (*id.*).

> 5 Corizon objects to PSOF ¶ 3 because it is supported by the declaration of Dr. [*8] Stokke, Larsgard's former treating physician in Norway; Corizon asserts that this declaration is improper, lacks foundation, and was not previously disclosed (Doc. 42 ¶ 3). There is nothing in *Rule 56* suggesting that affidavits used to oppose summary judgment must have been previously disclosed, and Corizon provides no legal authority to support that at summary judgment, Larsgard is limited to evidence disclosed during discovery. *See Fed. R. Civ. P. 56(c)(1)(A)* and *(4)*. Further, Dr. Stokke's declaration establishes personal knowledge and provides background regarding Larsgard's condition. *See Fed. R. Civ. P. 56(c)(4)*. The objection is overruled.

On March 4, 2013, Corizon assumed care and treatment of Larsgard when it replaced Wexford as the contracted entity with the State of Arizona to provide healthcare services to inmates (Doc. 32 at 4 n. 1).

Corizon states that Dr. Lewis attempted to wean Larsgard off of the high dose opioid analgesics and, in an April 2013 medical note, documented that Larsgard "is highly resistant to wean off opioid analgesics. My goal is gradual wean to lowest dose to maintain function" (DSOF ¶ 7). Larsgard states that Dr. Lewis advised him that Corizon ordered Dr. Lewis to discontinue morphine pain medication per its policy [*9] (PCSF ¶ 7).[6] Larsgard states that his pain medication regularly "ran out," which caused him to suffer severe bouts of pain (*id.*).

> 6 Corizon objects to PCSF ¶ 7 on the grounds that the assertions therein rely on Larsgard's declaration and "the declaration is disputed as it repeatedly makes statements without foundation and which contain hearsay" (Doc. 42 ¶ 4). Larsgard's statements satisfy the requirements of *Rule 56(c)(4)* (declaration must be made on personal knowledge and set out facts that would be admissible in evidence). Also, Corizon's objection that the declaration "repeatedly makes statements" lacking foundation and containing hearsay is too general. The Court will only consider specific objections to identified paragraphs within the declaration. *See Reinlasoder v. City of Colstrip*, CV-12-107-BLG, 2013 U.S. Dist. LEXIS 162351, 2013 WL 6048913,

at *7 (D. Mont. Nov. 14, 2013) (unpublished) ("objections [ ] must be stated with enough particularity to permit the Court to rule"). For these reasons, Corizon's objection is overruled.

Larsgard was not seen by Dr. Baaj for follow up until July 26, 2013 (DSOF ¶ 8; PCSF ¶ 8). At this appointment, Dr. Baaj noted that Larsgard had no post-op x-rays so he ordered that an x-ray and imagings "be performed immediately" and that a disk with [*10] the results be mailed to the hospital neurosurgery clinic (*id.*). He also ordered that Larsgard follow up with the neurosurgery clinic in 6 months for a cervical spine CT (DSOF ¶ 8).

On August 20, 2013, Larsgard saw prison Nurse Practitioner Richard Unger (DSOF ¶ 9). The medical record from this encounter reflects that the two discussed pain management and that Larsgard stated he felt his pain was under control with morphine sulfate (MS Contin) but he requested diazepam (Valium) for muscle spasms (Doc. 33, Ex. L (Doc. 33-1 at 23)). Larsgard was already on diazepam, but Unger increased the dosage and also submitted a consult request for a CT of the cervical spine in 6 months per Dr. Baaj's request (*id.*; PCSF ¶ 9). Thereafter, a "Utilization Management" physician reviewed Larsgard's medication history, determined that his medication combination with diazepam was a dangerous combination, and ordered that the dosage be reduced to prevent any adverse reaction (Doc. 40, Ex. 10 (Doc. 40-10 at 1)).

Defendant states that on August 22, 2013, x-rays were ordered for Larsgard's cervical spine, as requested by Dr. Baaj (DSOF ¶ 10).

On September 11, 2013, Larsgard met with Dr. Dimitri Catsaros at the [*11] prison; Dr. Catsaros ordered that the MS Contin (morphine) be continued (DSOF ¶ 11; PCSF ¶ 11).

On October 18, 2013, an MRI and CT of the cervical and thoracic spine were performed (DSOF ¶ 12; PCSF ¶ 12). The results, received on December 3, 2013, stated that the hospital chose not to perform the x-rays; that the CT scan showed a healed and aligned cervical spine and an unremarkable thoracic spine; and that metal placements in the spine created distortion and prevented an accurate MRI reading (DSOF ¶ 12).

On November 26, 2013, a neurological consult was ordered; the consult request was approved on December 5, 2013 by the Medical Director (DSOF ¶ 13).

On March 10, 2014, pursuant to the consult request, Larsgard saw Dr. Baaj, and Larsgard reported that his pain symptoms had improved (*id.*; PCSF ¶ 13). Dr. Baaj determined Larsgard had full range of motion of the neck without pain and "shows good alignment"; he noted that the C6/7 fracture had healed; he recommended pain management; and he noted that no further follow up was needed (DSOF ¶ 13 (in part) & Doc. 33, Ex. Q (Doc. 33-1 at 37)).

On March 18, 2014, Larsgard reported that he suffered a seizure and complained of neck pain; he was transferred [*12] to the University of Arizona Medical Center emergency facility (DSOF ¶ 14; PCSF ¶ 14). New CT scans were taken of Larsgard's head and neck, and all findings were negative for abnormalities (*id.*).

On March 27, 2014, Larsgard was transferred to the ADC Yuma facility (DSOF ¶ 15; PCSF ¶ 15).

On April 3, 2014, Larsgard saw Dr. Elijah Jordan at the prison (DSOF ¶ 16; PCSF ¶ 16 (in part)). Dr. Jordan advised Larsgard that it was time to wean off of the narcotic medications and replace them with non-narcotic medication; Larsgard was apprehensive to changes because his medications were at a comfortable level, although he also complained of neck pain (*id.*). Dr. Jordan ordered a tapering down of MS Contin over a period of 4 weeks and started prescriptions for Effexor and Baclofen, which act as muscle relaxants (DSOF ¶ 17).[7]

---

7 In PCSF ¶ 16, Larsgard asserts that Effexor is known to induce seizures, and asks the Court to take judicial notice of a website, "PDRhealth" at www.pdrhealth.com/drugs/effexor, and the information provided therein about Effexor. Corizon objects generally to PCSF ¶ 16; however, it is not clear whether it objects to this specific statement and website citation (Doc. 42 ¶ 11). [*13] Nonetheless, the Court will not consider the asserted fact because there is no statement or affidavit from a physician to support that Effexor was contraindicated for Larsgard due to the risk of seizures or any of the other risks listed. *See In re Homestore.com., Inc. v. Sec. Litig.*, 347 F. Supp. 2d 769, 782 (C.D. Cal. 2004) (finding print outs from a web site inadmissible at summary judgment because they were not properly authenticated by an affidavit

from someone with knowledge); *see also Barcamerica Int'l USA Trust v. Tyfield Imps., Inc., 289 F.3d 589, 593 n. 4 (9th Cir. 2002)* ("arguments and statements of counsel are not evidence") (internal quotation omitted).

On April 10, 2014, Larsgard saw Dr. Jordan again, at which time Larsgard reported that he did not feel well and he had suffered fainting episodes, and he had vomited after taking his medications (DSOF ¶ 18; PCSF ¶ 18). Dr. Jordan discontinued Effexor and replaced it with Depakote (DSOF ¶ 18). A couple days later, Dr. Jordan also prescribed Pamelor (DSOF ¶ 19). On April 16, 2014, a nurse notified Dr. Jordan that Larsgard refused his daily dosage of Depakote due to intolerance of the medication; therefore, Dr. Jordan continued tapering down the narcotics and discontinued Depakote and replaced it with Alph Lipoic Acid--a non-narcotic medication (*id.*). Dr. Jordan also prepared a consult request for [*14] a physician for pain management (*id.*).

On May 7, 2014, Larsgard again saw Dr. Jordan; Larsgard complained of pain, discomfort, and hypoglycemic symptoms (DSOF ¶ 20). The medical note from this appointment reflects that Dr. Jordan planned to prescribe Lyrica (Doc. 42, Ex. 2). The Lyrica prescription was submitted and, shortly thereafter, Dr. Jordan received the alternative recommendation of an equivalent medication, Neurontin (also known as Gabapentin) (Doc. 47 ¶ 2). On May 21, 2014, Dr. Jordan prescribed Neurontin/Gabapentin, a non-narcotic medication, as a replacement pain medication in lieu of Lyrica (*id.*; PCSF ¶ 19).

Meanwhile, on May 15, 2014, the request for an off-site consultation for pain management was approved (DSOF ¶ 22).

On May 21, 2014, Larsgard complained of an increased heart rate and appeared to have possible tachycardia issues, so the Pamelor prescription was immediately discontinued (DSOF ¶ 21). But Larsgard was administered Pamelor for two more days (PCSF ¶ 21).

On May 23, 2014, Larsgard began receiving the Neurontin/Gabapentin; however, it provided no relief (Doc. 40, Ex. 8, Larsgard Decl. ¶ 20 (Doc. 40-8 at 4)).

On June 3, 2014, pursuant to the off-site consultation [*15] request, Dr. Kevin S. Ladin, a physician board certified in pain medicine and physical medicine and rehabilitation, examined Larsgard (Doc. 40, Ex. 7, Ladin Decl. ¶¶ 1-2 (Doc. 40-7 at 1)). In his subsequent report, Dr. Ladin stated that Larsgard has suffered significant nerve damage and has incomplete spinal cord injury, resulting in a legitimate pain syndrome (*id.*, Ex. 6 at 6 (Doc. 40-6 at 6)). Dr. Ladin recommended that Larsgard receive treatment for chronic pain management consistent with the underlying pathophysiology of his pain, including a combination of a neuropathic analgesic medication like Neurontin combined with an antidepressant like Cymbalta (*id.*). He further stated that topical analgesics like Baclofen can be utilized as a muscle relaxant (*id.*). Dr. Laden recommended against the use of opioid or benzodiazepine medications because they have not been shown to be beneficial in neuropathic pain syndrome and have a high risk of dependency and addiction (*id.*). Dr. Ladin also opined that it is medically necessary for Larsgard to be treated by a pain management specialist with experience in spinal cord care and physical medicine (*id.*, Ex. 7, Ladin Decl. ¶¶ 3-4 (Doc. 40-7 at [*16] 1-2)).[8]

> 8   In its reply, Corizon argues that Dr. Ladin's declaration is deficient because it was not timely disclosed, it is improper as an expert opinion, and it is without foundation (Doc. 41 at 3-4). To the extent Corizon objects to Dr. Ladin's declaration, the objection is overruled. The declaration satisfies *Rule 56(c)(4)*, and prior disclosure of a declaration used to oppose summary judgment is not required. *See* n. 5. Also, Corizon is incorrect that it is not clear whether Dr. Ladin is referring to Larsgard's past or present treatment needs; his recommendations include no use of the past tense and are clearly referring to present treatment needs (Doc. 40-7 at 1-2).

In early June 2014, a prescription for Cymbalta was written; however, for reasons unknown, Larsgard did not receive this medication (Doc. 43 ¶ 4; Doc. 47 ¶ 4). Dr. Jordan has prescribed an equivalent medication, Prozac, which Larsgard is currently taking (Doc. 47 ¶ 4).

On July 9, 2014, Baclofen was discontinued (Doc. 43 ¶ 1; Doc. 47 ¶ 1). Corizon states that it was discontinued at Larsgard's request (Doc. 47 ¶ 1). Larsgard disputes that he ever requested to be taken off Baclofen as it was the only muscle spasm pain relief he was taking [*17] (Doc. 48 ¶ 2).

IV. Discussion

As mentioned, Corizon is a private entity contracted with the State to provide medical services to prisoners (*see* Doc. 33 at 3 n. 1). To support a § 1983 claim against a private entity performing a traditional public function, such as providing medical care to prisoners, a plaintiff must allege facts to support that his constitutional rights were violated as a result of a policy, decision, or custom promulgated or endorsed by the private entity. *See Tsao v. Desert Palace, Inc., 698 F.3d 1128, 1138-39 (9th Cir. 2012); Buckner v. Toro, 116 F.3d 450, 452 (11th Cir. 1997)*. A private entity is not liable simply because it employed individuals who allegedly violated a plaintiff's constitutional rights. *See Tsao, 698 F.3d at 1139*. Therefore, Corizon can only be held liable under § 1983 for its employees' civil rights deprivations if Larsgard can show that an official policy or custom caused the constitutional violation. *See George v. Sonoma Cnty. Sheriff's Dep't, 732 F. Supp. 2d 922 (N.D.Cal. 2010)* (inmate's survivors filed a § 1983 action for inadequate medical care, and court found that a private corporation could not be held liable for plaintiffs' injuries because they could not show that the violations occurred as a result of a policy, decision, or custom promulgated or endorsed by the private entity).

To maintain a claim against Corizon as an entity, Larsgard must meet the test articulated [*18] in *Monell v. Dep't of Soc. Servs., 436 U.S. 658, 690-94, 98 S. Ct. 2018, 56 L. Ed. 2d 611 (1978); see Tsao, 698 F.3d at 1139* (applying Monell to private entities). The requisite elements of a § 1983 claim against a private entity performing a state function are: (1) the plaintiff was deprived of a constitutional right; (2) the entity had a policy or custom; (3) the policy or custom amounted to deliberate indifference to the plaintiff's constitutional right; and (4) the policy or custom was the moving force behind the constitutional violation. *Mabe v. San Bernardino Cnty., Dep't of Pub. Soc. Servs., 237 F.3d 1101, 1110-11 (9th Cir. 2001)*. The limitations to liability established in *Monell* apply even where the plaintiff seeks only prospective relief and not money damages. *L.A. Cnty., Cal. v. Humphries, 562 U.S. 29, 131 S. Ct. 447, 450-51, 178 L. Ed. 2d 460 (2010)*.

A. Constitutional Deprivation

1. Governing Standard

Under the *Eighth Amendment* standard, a prisoner must demonstrate "deliberate indifference to serious medical needs." *Jett v. Penner, 439 F.3d 1091, 1096 (9th Cir. 2006)* (citing *Estelle v. Gamble, 429 U.S. 97, 104, 97 S. Ct. 285, 50 L. Ed. 2d 251 (1976))*. There are two prongs to the deliberate-indifference analysis: an objective standard and a subjective standard. First, a prisoner must show a "serious medical need." *Jett, 439 F.3d at 1096* (citations omitted). A "'serious' medical need exists if the failure to treat a prisoner's condition could result in further significant injury or the 'unnecessary and wanton infliction of pain.'" *McGuckin v. Smith, 974 F.2d 1050, 1059-60 (9th Cir. 1992)*, overruled on other grounds, *WMX Techs., Inc. v. Miller, 104 F.3d 1133, 1136 (9th Cir. 1997)* (en banc) (internal citation omitted). Examples of indications that a prisoner [*19] has a serious medical need include "[t]he existence of an injury that a reasonable doctor or patient would find important and worthy of comment or treatment; the presence of a medical condition that significantly affects an individual's daily activities; or the existence of chronic and substantial pain." *McGuckin, 974 F.2d at 1059-60*.

Second, a prisoner must show that the defendant's response to that need was deliberately indifferent. *Jett, 439 F.3d at 1096*. An official acts with deliberate indifference if he "knows of and disregards an excessive risk to inmate health or safety; the official must both be aware of facts from which the inference could be drawn that a substantial risk of serious harm exists, and he must also draw the inference." *Farmer, 511 U.S. at 837*. "Prison officials are deliberately indifferent to a prisoner's serious medical needs when they deny, delay, or intentionally interfere with medical treatment," *Hallett v. Morgan, 296 F.3d 732, 744 (9th Cir.2002)* (internal citations and quotation marks omitted), or when they fail to respond to a prisoner's pain or possible medical need. *Jett, 439 F.3d at 1096*. But the deliberate-indifference doctrine is limited; an inadvertent failure to provide adequate medical care or negligence in diagnosing or treating a medical condition does not support an *Eighth Amendment* claim. *Wilhelm v. Rotman, 680 F.3d 1113, 1122 (9th Cir. 2012)* (citations omitted). [*20] Further, a mere difference in medical opinion does not establish deliberate indifference. *Jackson v. McIntosh, 90 F.3d 330, 332 (9th Cir. 1996)*.

Where the plaintiff seeks injunctive relief to prevent a substantial risk of serious injury from becoming actual harm, the deliberate indifference determination is based on the defendant's current conduct. *Farmer, 511 U.S. at 845*. Thus, to survive summary judgment, the plaintiff "must come forward with evidence from which it can be inferred that the defendant-officials were at the time suit was filed, and are at the time of summary judgment, knowingly and unreasonably disregarding an objectively intolerable risk of harm, and that they will continue to do so[.]" *Id. at 846*.

Even if deliberate indifference is shown, to support an *Eighth Amendment* claim, the prisoner must demonstrate harm caused by the indifference. *Jett, 439 F.3d at 1096*; *see Hunt v. Dental Dep't, 865 F.2d 198, 200 (9th Cir. 1989)* (delay in providing medical treatment does not constitute *Eighth Amendment* violation unless delay was harmful). And to support a preliminary injunction for specific medical treatment, the plaintiff must demonstrate ongoing harm or the present threat of irreparable injury. *See Conn. v. Mass., 282 U.S. 660, 674, 51 S. Ct. 286, 75 L. Ed. 602 (1931)* (an injunction is only appropriate "to prevent existing or presently threatened injuries"); *see Caribbean Marine Servs. Co. v. Baldrige, 844 F.2d 668, 674 (9th Cir. 1988)*.

2. Deliberate Indifference

Corizon makes no argument that Larsgard's [*21] condition does not constitute a serious medical need (*see* Doc. 32). Indeed, the record reflects that Larsgard's condition causes him chronic and severe pain and that medical personnel found his condition worthy of attention and treatment. *See McGuckin, 974 F.2d at 1059-60*. The analysis therefore turns on whether the response to Larsgard's serious medical need was deliberately indifferent; specifically, whether the failure to provide pain management treatment with a specialist and whether the changes to and discontinuation of certain medications amounts to deliberate indifference.

Refusing to follow the advice of a treating specialist may evidence deliberate indifference. *See Snow v. McDaniel, 681 F.3d 978, 988 (9th Cir. 2012)* (where the treating physician and specialist recommended surgery, a reasonable jury could conclude that it was medically unacceptable for the non-treating, non-specialist physicians to deny recommendations for surgery), overruled in part on other grounds, *Peralta v. Dillard, 744 F.3d 1076, 1082-83 (9th Cir. 2014)*; *Jones v. Simek, 193 F.3d 485, 490 (7th Cir. 1999)* (the defendant physician's refusal to follow the advice of treating specialists could constitute deliberate indifference to serious medical needs). In addition, a failure to competently treat a serious medical condition, even if some treatment is prescribed, may constitute deliberate indifference [*22] in a particular case. *Ortiz v. City of Imperial, 884 F.2d 1312, 1314 (9th Cir. 1989)* ("access to medical staff is meaningless unless that staff is competent and can render competent care"); *see Estelle, 429 U.S. at 105 & n. 10* (the treatment received by a prisoner can be so bad that the treatment itself manifests deliberate indifference); *Lopez v. Smith, 203 F.3d 1122, 1132 (9th Cir. 2000)* (prisoner does not have to prove that he was completely denied medical care).

a. Post-Surgery Treatment

The Court first addresses Larsgard's past treatment and whether it constituted deliberately indifferent care. The undisputed facts show that in January 2013, Larsgard underwent emergency surgery on his spine (Doc. 33, DSOF ¶ 3); the surgeon, Dr. Baaj, directed that Larsgard should return for follow up within 3 weeks after surgery (Doc. 31, Ex. 1 (Doc. 13-1 at 3)); yet, Larsgard was not taken for his first follow up appointment until July 26, 2013--more than six months later and more than four months after Corizon assumed care for Larsgard (Doc. 33, DSOF ¶ 8). In addition, x-rays that Dr. Baaj specifically requested be performed before the July 26 follow up appointment were not done (Doc. 40, Ex. 9 at 5 (Doc. 40-9 at 5)). And, although Dr. Baaj recommended at the July 26 follow up that x-rays and imagings "be performed immediately" [*23] and the results mailed to him, the imagings were not done until October 2013 (*id.* at 12 (Doc. 40-9 at 12); Doc. 33, DSOF ¶ 12). Also, Dr. Baaj recommended pain management post surgery (Doc. 40-1 at 10), and one post-surgical note documenting pain management recommendations states "f/u [with] outpatient chronic pain MD" (*id.* at 25 (Jan. 3, 2013 post-op pain management consult med. record)), which, when making all inferences in Larsgard's favor, supports that follow up with a pain management physician or specialist was recommended. Even assuming that a specialist in pain management was not recommended, as Corizon argues, its own asserted facts show that the first pain management appointment or "discussion" was not until August 20, 2013 with Nurse Practitioner Unger (Doc. 33, DSOF ¶ 9).

In light of these substantial delays in following the treating specialist's recommendations, there are material factual disputes whether, in 2013, medical staff was deliberately indifferent to Larsgard's serious medical needs following his surgery. But, as stated, even if deliberate indifference is shown, to maintain his *Eighth Amendment* claim, Larsgard must demonstrate harm caused by the indifference. *Jett, 439 F.3d at 1096*.

At his March 10, 2014 follow up appointment, [*24] Dr. Baaj noted that Larsgard's pain was improved and he had good alignment, no hardware complications, and full range of motion in his neck without pain (Doc. 33, Ex. Q (Doc. 33-1 at 37)). Larsgard acknowledges that despite the delays, he did not suffer complications post surgery, which he attributes to Dr. Baaj and the hospital staff (Doc. 39 at 11). But the infliction of pain can constitute an *Eighth Amendment* violation even if a delay in treatment does not impact further treatment. *See McGuckin, 974 F.2d at 1060*. Larsgard avers that upon his release from the rehabilitation center in February 2013, his pain control was "very good" due to the combination of medications he was receiving (Doc. 40, Ex. 8, Larsgard Decl. ¶¶ 2-3 (Doc. 40-8 at 1)). He states that in June 2013, his Clonazepam was discontinued and he began suffering severe muscle spasms that prevented sleep for more than a couple of hours at a time for several weeks until he was prescribed diazepam (*id*. ¶ 6). At his July 26, 2013 appointment with Dr. Baaj, Larsgard had progressive weakness and increasing pain in his neck that prevented sleep for more than an hour at a time (Doc. 13-1 at 14). But at his August 20, 2013 appointment with the Nurse Practitioner, Larsgard [*25] reported that his pain was manageable (Doc. 33, DSOF ¶ 9; Doc. 40, PCSF ¶ 9). And Larsgard declared that prior to his transfer to Yuma in March 2014, his "level of pain control had been acceptable for most of the day," although there were 2-3 hours gaps between his morphine doses when pain control was inadequate and the diazepam dosage was too low to entirely control muscle spasms (*id*. ¶ 7).

These facts demonstrate that there was a period in June-July 2013 when changes to Larsgard's medication resulted in increased muscle spasms and increased neck pain; however, Larsgard's own averments establish that before he moved to the Yuma facility in March 2014, his pain was, for the most part, manageable. Consequently, although the record supports a material factual dispute whether medical personnel were deliberately indifferent to Larsgard's serious medical needs after surgery when they delayed treatment recommended by Dr. Baaj, because Larsgard cannot show that he suffered harm as a result, his *Eighth Amendment* claim fails as to his past treatment.

b. Current Treatment

To maintain his *Eighth Amendment* claim for injunctive relief--specifically, his request for specialist care for pain management--Larsgard must show that he is [*26] currently subject to deliberately indifferent treatment and that he is suffering ongoing harm as a result. *See Farmer, 511 U.S. at 846*.

Corizon asserts that since Dr. Baaj released Larsgard from further follow up care, it began transitioning Larsgard to non-narcotic medications for his own health and well-being (Doc. 32 at 12). In support of its claim that this course of treatment is adequate, Corizon proffers the March 20, 2014 expert opinion of Dr. William R. Stevens, a board certified orthopedic surgeon, who reviewed Larsgard's medical records (Doc. 33, Ex. Z (Doc. 33-1 at 74-75)). Dr. Stevens opines that Larsgard's current pain medication regimen is more than adequate for his condition and that "pain management consultation might be medically reasonable"; however, it is "not medically imperative unless" efforts to taper the opioid medications prove unsuccessful (*id*.). Corizon also asserts that it referred Larsgard to a pain specialist, Dr. Ladin, on June 3, 2014,[9] and Dr. Ladin agreed that Larsgard should be weaned off opioid or narcotic pain medications (Doc. 41 at 4). Corizon maintains that it is now following Dr. Ladin's recommendations; thus, Larsgard cannot show that the current course of treatment [*27] is medically unacceptable (Doc. 41 at 4, 6).

> 9   The Court notes that although Corizon referred Larsgard to a pain specialist on June 3, 2014, Corizon makes no argument that the request for an injunction for pain management specialist care is moot (*see* Doc. 41 at 2, 4). Instead, Corizon argues that specialist care for pain management is not required and that

pain management provided by its licensed health staff is medically appropriate (*see* Doc. 32 at 3, 9, 11-12; Doc. 41 at 1-2; Doc. 42 ¶ 2). Further, Dr. Ladin stated in his report he was asked to serve as a consultant specifically to comment on whether Larsgard requires MS Contin and diazepam (Doc. 40-6 at 6). And, as stated, Corizon argues that Dr. Ladin's separate declaration is improper and lacks foundation because it contains "no statement as to whether the nature of care Dr. Ladin is now recommending is relevant to now or some, if any, times in the past" (Doc. 41 at 4). Corizon's arguments suggest that Dr. Ladin's consult was limited in scope and does not represent that specialist care will be provided in the future; therefore, the Court finds that the June 3, 2014 appointment with Dr. Ladin does not moot Larsgard's request for pain [*28] management specialist care.

In response, Larsgard contends that Corizon's staff is not qualified to address his complicated medical needs (Doc. 39 at 7, 11). In his declaration, Larsgard states that since he arrived in Yuma in March 2014, his morphine dosages have not been provided and he has been given various ineffective medications (Doc. 40, Ex. 8, Larsgard Decl. ¶ 9 (Doc. 40-8 at 2)). The record shows that some medications provided to Larsgard caused potentially harmful side effects, including hypoglycemia and tachycardia issues, which required replacement medications (Doc. 33, DSOF ¶¶ 20-21).

Larsgard also contends that his pain is currently not manageable. At the time of his declaration--May 31, 2014--Larsgard reported severe pain that prevents him from sleeping more than 10 minutes at a time and interferes with most daily activities (Doc. 40, Ex. 8 ¶ 10). At his June 3, 2014 appointment, Larsgard reported ongoing, severe pain in his neck, left shoulder, and upper arm, and he stated that the pain is sharp, stabbing, and aching in quality (*id.*, Ex. 6 (Doc. 40-6 at 3)). He further reported that his pain is only partially relieved with MS Contin and that nothing else has helped (*id* [*29] .). The Court also notes Dr. Ladin's June 2014 diagnosis that Larsgard suffered significant nerve damage and has legitimate pain syndrome and components of both nociceptive and neuropathic pain (Doc. 40, Ex. 6 at 6 (Doc. 40-6 at 6)). The inference from this evidence is that Larsgard is currently suffering harm.

With respect to the need for specialist care, Larsgard submits his own expert opinion, that of Dr. Harvinder S. Bedi, an orthopedic spine surgeon, who reviewed Larsgard's medical records in February 2014 (Doc. 39 at 7, 11; Doc. 40, Ex. 16 (Doc. 40-16 at 1-2)). Dr. Bede opined that it is imperative Larsgard obtain treatment from a qualified pain management specialist due to his chronic high dose pain medication requirement (Doc. 40-16 at 1-2). Larsgard also relies on Dr. Ladin's opinion that it is medically necessary for Larsgard to be treated by a pain management specialist with experience in spinal cord care and that a nurse practitioner or general practitioner providing pain management is inappropriate given Larsgard's complex condition (Doc. 40, Ex. 7, Ladin Decl. ¶¶ 3-4 (Doc. 40-7 at 1-2)). The Court notes that unlike Drs. Stevens and Bedi, who only reviewed Larsgard's medical [*30] records, Dr. Ladin reviewed the medical records *and* conducted an in-person interview and physical examination of Larsgard (Doc. 33-1 at 74; Doc. 40-16 at 1; Doc. 40-6 at 1-6). *See Snow, 681 F.3d at 987-88* (noting that the physicians who denied recommended surgery for the prisoner had not examined or treated the prisoner).

On Corizon's motion, the Court must make all inferences in Larsgard's favor. *Anderson, 477 U.S. at 255*. When doing so, Drs. Bedi and Ladin's opinions support the inference that pain management care by a specialist is medically necessary. At summary judgment, the opinion of Corizon's expert, Dr. Stevens, does not overcome this inference. *See Snow, 681 F.3d at 988, 992* (finding that the district court improperly concluded that there was a mere disagreement of medical opinion and, in doing so, failed to identify the triable issues of fact whether the defendants delayed appropriate medical treatment or whether their course of treatment was medically unacceptable). Because the denial of medically necessary treatment constitutes deliberate indifference, *see Estelle, 429 U.S. at 104-05*, there exists a triable issue of fact concerning whether Corizon's course of treating Larsgard's current pain needs with non-specialist medical personnel is "medically unacceptable under the [*31] circumstances" and chosen "in conscious disregard of an excessive risk to [Largard's] health." *See Jackson, 90 F.3d at 332*.

B. Policy or Custom Amounting to Deliberate Indifference

As discussed above, whether there is a constitutional violation--in this case, deliberate indifference to serious medical needs--is the first of four elements to be considered when determining whether an entity is liable under § 1983. Because there is a material factual dispute on that first element, the Court must consider whether

Corizon had a policy or custom and, if so, whether that policy or custom amounted to deliberate indifference and was the moving force behind the constitutional violation. *Mabe, 237 F.3d at 1110-11*; *see Tsao, 698 F.3d at 1139* (private entity liable under *§ 1983* only if constitutional violation caused by a policy).

Corizon does not present any argument regarding the policy requirement, nor does it show that Larsgard lacks evidence to support this element of his claim. *See Nissan, 210 F.3d at 1102*. In his declaration, Larsgard makes a few allegations regarding a policy (*see* Doc. 40, Ex. 8, Larsgard Decl. ¶¶ 4, 19 (Doc. 40-8 at 1, 3); Doc. 43, Ex. 1, Larsgard Supp. Decl. ¶¶ 4-5 (Doc. 43-2 at 1-2)); however, he was not on notice that he must present facts and evidence of a policy or custom [*32] that amounted to deliberate indifference. *See Katz v. Children's Hosp. of Orange Cnty., 28 F.3d 1520, 1534 (9th Cir. 1994)* (the nonmovant fails to satisfy its burden to show that there is a genuine issue for trial only if the movant has placed it on proper notice); *Evans v. United Air Lines, Inc., 986 F.2d 942, 945 (5th Cir. 1993)* (where the defendant's summary judgment motion did not address many of the plaintiffs' claims, the plaintiffs were not on notice as to those claims). Accordingly, Corizon fails to meet its initial summary judgment burden on this portion of Larsgard's claim.

In light of the material factual dispute regarding whether there is deliberate indifference to Larsgard's current serious medical need, the Motion for Summary Judgment will be denied.

V. New Summary Judgment Motion Deadline

A district court may enter summary judgment on grounds not raised by a party if it gives notice and a reasonable time to respond. *Fed. R. Civ. P. 56(f)(2)*. In this case, evidence and briefing regarding whether there exists a policy or custom and whether that policy or custom amounts to deliberate indifference could be dispositive of the *Eighth Amendment* claim and should be considered before trial. The Court will therefore permit Corizon to file a new summary judgment motion addressing the remaining elements for a *§ 1983* claim against an entity; specifically, (1) whether [*33] Corizon has a policy or custom; (2) whether the policy or custom amounts to deliberate indifference to Larsgard's constitutional right; and (3) whether the policy or custom was the moving force behind the constitutional violation. *Mabe, 237 F.3d at 1110-11*; *see Hoffman v. Tonnemacher, 593 F.3d 908, 911-12 (9th Cir. 2010)* (a district court has discretion to permit successive motions for summary judgment).

APPENDIX D

CHARLES ISELEY, Appellant v. JEFFREY BEARD; ROBERT BITNER; KENNETH KYLER; FRANK GILLIS; WILMA SEWELL; KANDIS DASCANI; JOSEPH KORT, DIANA BANEY; PATRICIA EVERHART; PATRICIA YARGER; DAWN MILLS, Physician Asst.; PAUL ROEMER; MARY SHOWALTER; KILE; CYNTHIA STEVENS; JOHN SIDLER; PHS, INC.; ASG, INC.; WEXFORD HEALTH SERVICES, INC.

NO. 06-2465

UNITED STATES COURT OF APPEALS FOR THE THIRD CIRCUIT

237 Fed. Appx. 735; 2007 U.S. App. LEXIS 15376

May 4, 2007, Submitted Under Third Circuit LAR 34.1(a)
June 27, 2007, Filed

NOTICE: NOT PRECEDENTIAL OPINION UNDER THIRD CIRCUIT INTERNAL OPERATING PROCEDURE RULE 5.7. SUCH OPINIONS ARE NOT REGARDED AS PRECEDENTS WHICH BIND THE COURT.

PLEASE REFER TO FEDERAL RULES OF APPELLATE PROCEDURE RULE 32.1 GOVERNING THE CITATION TO UNPUBLISHED OPINIONS.

SUBSEQUENT HISTORY: Motion denied by *Iseley v. Beard*, 2007 U.S. Dist. LEXIS 90280 (M.D. Pa., Dec. 6, 2007)

PRIOR HISTORY: [**1]
On Appeal From the United States District Court For the Middle District of Pennsylvania. (D.C. Civ. No. 02-cv-02006). District Judge: Honorable Yvette Kane.
Iseley v. Talaber, 232 Fed. Appx. 120, 2007 U.S. App. LEXIS 12160 (3d Cir. Pa., 2007)

COUNSEL: CHARLES ISELEY, Appellant, Pro se, Fayette SCI, LaBelle, PA.

For JEFFREY BEARD, ROBERT BITNER, KENNETH KYLER, FRANK GILLIS, WILMA SEWELL, KANDIS DASCANI, DIANA BANEY, PATRICIA EVERHART, PATRICIA YARGER, MARY SHOWALTER, JOHN SIDLER, Appellees: Raymond W. Dorian, Pennsylvania Department of Corrections, Office Chief Counsel, Camp Hill, PA.

For JOSEPH KORT, PHS INC, ASG INC, Appellees: A. Tracey Campbell, White & Williams, Berwyn, PA.

For DAWN MILLS, PAUL ROEMER, WEXFORD HEALTH SER, Appellees: Samuel H. Foreman, Weber, Gallagher, Simpsons, Stapleton, Fires & Newby, Pittsburgh, PA.

JUDGES: Before: SLOVITER, MCKEE AND AMBRO, CIRCUIT JUDGES.

OPINION

[*736] PER CURIAM

Charles Iseley appeals from the order of the United States District Court for the Middle District of Pennsylvania granting summary judgment in favor of some defendants and dismissing his action as to the remaining defendants. We will affirm in part, vacate in part, and remand the matter for further proceedings.

The parties are well-acquainted with the history of this case, so we will recount the background [**2] only as relevant to this appeal. Iseley is currently incarcerated at the State Correctional Institution ("SCI") Fayette [*737] at LaBelle, Pennsylvania. He suffers from a number of medical conditions, including Hepatitis-C ("HCV"), fibromyalgia, chronic fatigue syndrome, and rheumatoid arthritis. In 2000, Iseley filed a civil rights action under *42 U.S.C. § 1983* in the United States District Court for the Eastern District of Pennsylvania. He alleged, *inter alia*, that the failure of the defendants to offer him treatment for HCV constituted cruel and unusual punishment. In addition, Iseley claimed that the denial of medical care was in retaliation for having filed grievances and lawsuits against prison officials and employees. The defendants in that action included prison officials from SCI-Mahanoy and SCI-Coal Township, certain prison medical providers, and the former Secretary of the Department of Corrections ("DOC"). After the DOC changed its policy concerning HCV treatment, Iseley unsuccessfully sought a preliminary injunction to compel the DOC to provide him with prescription drug treatment for HCV, despite Iseley's refusals to consent to psychological testing and limited disclosure as [**3] required by the DOC's treatment protocols. The District Court granted summary judgment to the defendants, and we affirmed. See *Iseley v. Dragovich*, Civ. No. 00-cv-04839 (E.D. Pa. Feb. 28, 2005), *aff'd 90 Fed. Appx. 577, 2004 WL 229449 (3d Cir. 2004)* (not precedential).

Meanwhile, in 2002, Iseley filed the complaint in this action, as amended in September 2003. He named as defendants DOC officials and employees (both past and present), SCI-Coal Township and SCI-Huntington officials and personnel, ("Commonwealth defendants"), prison medical providers from SCI-Huntington, [1] again alleging deliberate indifference to his medical needs in denial of treatment for his HCV while housed at those institutions. Once again, Iseley's lawsuit is focused on the defendants' denial of medical treatment because he withheld his consent to the psychological testing aspect of the DOC HCV protocol. His complaint listed numerous claims, including that the failure of the defendants to treat his HCV, fibromyalgia, chronic fatigue syndrome, and rheumatoid arthritis constituted cruel and unusual punishment in violation of the *Eighth* and *Fourteenth Amendments*; that he was denied medical treatment in violation of [**4] the Americans with Disabilities Act ("ADA"); that the refusal to treat his HCV was in retaliation for his failure to consent to psychological treatment; and that he was denied medical treatment in violation of his Equal Protection rights. Iseley also alleged various state law claims. Iseley sought damages and injunctive relief in the form of medical treatment.

> 1   Among the prison medical providers are defendants Dawn Mills, a physician's assistant, and Dr. Paul Roemer, a physician. They were employed by defendant Wexford Health Sources, Inc. ("Wexford"), the former contractual health care provider at SCI-Huntington.

Iseley filed a motion for appointment of counsel, which the District Court conditionally granted on March 24, 2004, indicating that the conditional order would be revoked if counsel could not be found to represent Iseley. Defendants Mills, Roemer, and Wexford filed a motion for summary judgment, arguing that they did not violate Iseley's *Eighth Amendment* rights. Rather, they contended that Iseley refused to cooperate with health care providers in following the diagnostic and classification protocols, including the required psychological screening, as was required of all inmates [**5] seeking HCV treatment. They also contended that Iseley's claims were barred by the doctrine of collateral estoppel. In support, they cited Iseley's previous litigation in *Iseley v. Dragovich*, *supra*, asserting that Iseley previously [*738] unsuccessfully litigated the identical issues regarding the denial of HCV treatment, the validity of the DOC HCV protocol, the psychiatric screening requirement, and the consent form requirement.

On February 28, 2005, the District Court granted the motion for summary judgment filed by defendants Mills, Roemer, and Wexford, concluding that collateral estoppel applied to bar Iseley's complaint. In addition, the District Court dismissed the amended complaint under *28 U.S.C. § 1915(e)(2)(B)(ii)* for failure to state a claim as to the remaining defendants. The District Court denied Iseley's motions to alter and to reconsider the judgment. Iseley appeals.

We have appellate jurisdiction pursuant to *28 U.S.C. § 1291*. We exercise plenary review over a District Court's grant of summary judgment and apply the same test applied by the District Court. *Saldana v. Kmart Corp., 260 F.3d 228, 231, 43 V.I. 361 (3d Cir. 2001)*. Summary judgment is proper when, viewing the evidence in the light [**6] most favorable to the nonmovant, there is no genuine issue of material fact and the moving party is entitled to judgment as a matter of law. *Id. at 232; Fed. R. Civ. P. 56(c)*. We will view the facts in the light most favorable to the nonmoving party, and we will draw all inferences in that party's favor. *See Reitz v. County of Bucks, 125 F.3d 139, 143 (3d Cir. 1997)*. Similarly, our review of the District Court's dismissal for failure to state a claim under *section 1915(e)* is plenary. *Allah v. Seiverling, 229 F.3d 220, 223 (3d Cir. 2000)*. We may affirm the District Court on any ground supported by the record. *Tourscher v. McCullough, 184 F.3d 236, 240 (3d Cir. 1999)*.

Iseley's HCV-Related Claims

The appellees argue that collateral estoppel bars the relitigation of Iseley's claims regarding the denial of HCV treatment, the DOC HCV protocol, and the required psychiatric screening and consent forms. For substantially the same reasons stated by the District Court, we agree. The District Court considered the factors we have applied in determining whether collateral estoppel applies: (1) whether the identical issue was presented in a previous action; (2) whether the prior action resulted in [**7] a final judgment on the merits; (3) whether the party against whom collateral estoppel is asserted was a party or in privity to a party to the prior case; and (4) whether the party against whom the doctrine is asserted had a full and fair opportunity to litigate the issue previously. *See Temple Univ. v. White, 941 F.2d 201, 212 (3d Cir. 1991)*. With respect to the *Iseley v. Dragovich* case, of Iseley's HCV issues concerning the alleged denial of care relating to the DOC protocol and screening procedures are identical to the issues presented in *Iseley v. Dragovich*, which resulted in a final merits determination. Iseley was (obviously) a party to his prior case, and he had a full and fair opportunity in his prior case to litigate the issue. [2] We are unpersuaded by Iseley's arguments attempting to differentiate the present case from the *Iseley v. Dragovich* case concerning his HCV treatment claims. [3]

2   We specifically noted that Iseley had ample opportunity to litigate his previous case. *Iseley v. Dragovich, 90 Fed. Appx. at 582, 2004 WL 229449, at *3*.

3

Iseley also argues that the Commonwealth defendants should be precluded from raising collateral estoppel because they attempted to remove [**8] to federal court Iseley's related state court case, arguing that Iseley's HCV claims must be addressed in a federal civil action. Iseley attached to his brief a copy of the District Court's order in *Iseley v. Beard*, No. 02-cv-00180 (M.D. Pa. Sept. 30, 2002), dated September 30, 2002, denying removal and remanding the matter to state court. Iseley states that he voluntarily withdrew that action and proceeded to file in federal court. Even assuming Iseley's account of this history is correct, we are unpersuaded that the Commonwealth's collateral estoppel argument is nullified. The Commonwealth's removal petition was filed well before judgment was entered on Iseley's claim in the *Iseley v. Dragovich* matter.

Iseley's Remaining Claims

Iseley argues that the District Court did not address his remaining claims (*e.g.*, the alleged failures to treat his other illnesses; the alleged violations of the Americans with Disabilities Act and his [*739] rights under the *Equal Protection clause* and his state law claims). Indeed, it appears from the record that defendants Mills, Roemer, and Wexford did not argue that these claims were precluded by collateral estoppel in their summary judgment motion, and the [**9] District Court's memorandum does not address the claims as they pertain to any of the defendants. Iseley also argues that the District Court should not have dismissed his complaint for failure to state a claim. We observe that the procedural history in the District Court proceedings is somewhat puzzling. For instance, the record indicates that Iseley paid the filing fee for his civil action and apparently was not proceeding *in forma pauperis*. Yet as noted above, in addition to granting summary judgment, the District Court dismissed Iseley's complaint against the other defendants, under the provisions of *28 U.S.C. 1915(e)(2)(B)(ii)*, discussing only the denial of HCV treatment without a psychological evaluation. We have noted that *section 1915(e)(2)* only applies to litigants proceeding *in forma pauperis*. *See Grayson v. Mayview State Hosp., 293 F.3d 103, 109-10, n.10 (3d Cir. 2002)* (citing *Benson v. O'Brian, 179 F.3d 1014, 1016-17 (6th Cir. 1999)*). In addition, the District Court conditionally granted Iseley's motion for appointment of counsel. In so doing, the District Court stated that it had considered the factors of *Tabron v. Grace, 6 F.3d 147, 155-57 (3d Cir. 1993)*, and found that [**10] Iseley's complaint, insofar as it related to his Eighth Amendment medical treatment claims,[4] had satisfied the threshold requirement of having potential merit. (District Court March 24, 2004 Mem. at 3.) None of Iseley's other claims are discussed, and it is unclear whether the District Court differentiated Iseley's medical claims regarding HCV from his claims regarding other ailments. Because the District Court record provides no clear indication regarding the disposition of Iseley's remaining claims, and in light of the somewhat irregular procedural history, we will remand the matter.

3 The District Court's memorandum identified that the complaint alleged the denial of medical care for "chronic liver disease and other serious ailments," and that a "wide range of medical problems. . . including 'chronic hepatitis c/cirrhosis'" was at issue. (District Court March 24, 2004 Mem. at 1-2.)

REMEDY AND REDEMPTION
TABLE OF AUTHORITIES

Cases

. Jeffes v Barnes, 208 F.3d 49, 57 (2nd Cir. 2000) 2
. Robert P. Torres, Plaintiff, vs. Charles Ryan, et al., Defendants.No. CV 12-0006-PHX-JAT (DKD)UNITED STATES DISTRICT COURT FOR THE DISTRICT OF ARIZONA 21, 51
Ace B. Freemon, Plaintiff, vs. Charles Ryan, et al., Defendants No. CV 09-1717-PHX-JAT (JRI) UNITED STATES DISTRICT COURT FOR THE DISTRICT OF ARIZONA 7
AMIN RAHMAN SHAKUR, Plaintiff/Appellant, v. DORA B. SCHRIRO; CHARLES RYAN, Defendants/Appellees.No. 1 CA-CV 10-0530COURT OF APPEALS OF ARIZONA, DIVISION ONE, DEPARTMENT........................ 9
AMMAR DEAN HALLOUM, Plaintiff, vs. CHARLES RYAN, et al., Defendants.No. CV 11-0097-PHX-RCB (JRI) UNITED STATES DISTRICT COURT FOR THE DISTRICT OF ARIZONA... 6
Andre Almond Dennison, Plaintiff, v. Charles L. Ryan, et al., Defendants. No. CV-13-01925-PHX-SPL (ESW) UNITED STATES DISTRICT COURT FOR THE DISTRICT OF ARIZONA 6
Anthony Merrick, Plaintiff, vs. Charles L. Ryan, et al., Defendants.No. CV 13-2386-PHX-RCB (BSB) 4
Ardra Young, Plaintiff, v. LaToya Jackson, Vindha Jayawardena, Michigan Department of Corrections, and Corizon Health, Inc., Defendants.Case No. 12-cv-12751 UNITED STATES DISTRICT COURT FOR THE EASTERN DISTRICT OF MICHIGAN, SOUTHERN DIVISION 28
Barry Northcross Patterson, Plaintiff, vs. Charles L. Ryan, et al., Defendants. No. CV 05-1159-PHX-RCB (SPL) UNITED STATES DISTRICT COURT FOR THE DISTRICT OF ARIZONA 2
BETH E. BRONDAS, Plaintiff, v. CORIZON HEALTH, INC., Defendant.CIVIL ACTION NO. 7:14-CV-00369 27
BRIAN GRIMALDI, Plaintiff, v. CORIZON, INC., f/k/a CORRECTIONAL MEDICAL SERVICES, INC., and ANNIE GREY, Defendants. CIVIL ACTION NO. 10-1686 (JEI/JS) UNITED STATES DISTRICT COURT FOR THE DISTRICT OF NEW JERSEY 34
CARL RUPERT SMITH, #137 787, Plaintiff, v. CORIZON HEALTH SERVICES, et al., Defendants. CIVIL ACTION NO. 2:15-CV-20-MHT UNITED STATES DISTRICT COURT FOR THE MIDDLE DISTRICT OF ALABAMA, NORTHERN DIVISION 33
Cedric Kushner Promotions Ltd. Vs. King, 533 U.S. 158, 161 (2001)..23, 26, 41
CHARLES ISELEY, Appellant v. JEFFREY BEARD; ROBERT BITNER; KENNETH KYLER; FRANK GILLIS; WILMA SEWELL; KANDIS DASCANI; JOSEPH KORT, DIANA BANEY; PATRICIA EVERHART; PATRICIA YARGER; DAWN MILLS, Physician Asst.; PAUL ROEMER; MARY SHOWALTER; KILE; CYNTHIA STEVENS; JOHN SIDLER; PHS, INC.; ASG, INC.; WEXFORD HEALTH SERVICES, INC. NO. 06-2465 UNITED STATES COURT OF APPEALS FOR THE THIRD CIRCUIT 20, 50
CHARLES TONGE, Plaintiff, v. CORIZON HEALTH SERVICES, INC. and THE CITY OF NEW YORK, Defendants. No. 14-CV-3954 (RA) UNITED STATES DISTRICT COURT FOR THE SOUTHERN DISTRICT OF NEW YORK.................... 34
Chew v Gates, 27 F.3d 1432, 1445 (9th Cir. 1994).. 2
CHRISTINA BOBBIN, in her capacity as Plenary Guardian of Carlo Daniel Laudadio, an incapacitated adult, Plaintiff, v. CORIZON HEALTH, INC., NATALIA SAUNDERS, H.S.A., JANICE STEPNOSKI, L.C.S.W., WALTER CARL MORRIS, RN, NOEL DOMINGUEZ, M.D., ANDREW PAUL SAFRON, III, D.O., SVOBODA MARIA HOLT, LMHC, JANET JOAN MEMOLI, RN, MIKE SCOTT, in his official capacity as Lee County Sheriff, PAUL A. PAVESE, Sergeant, and RODNEY K. PAYNE, Deputy, individually, Defendants. Case No: 2:14-cv-158-FtM-29MRM UNITED STATES DISTRICT COURT FOR THE MIDDLE DISTRICT OF FLORIDA, FORT MYERS DIVISION 39
CHRISTOPHER LEWIS, Plaintiff, v. CORIZON HEALTH CARE, et al., Defendants.CIVIL NO. 4:14-CV-00885 UNITED STATES DISTRICT COURT FOR THE MIDDLE DISTRICT OF PENNSYLVANIA... 33
City Of Vernon v Southern Cal. Edison. Co. 955 F.2d 1361, 1371 (9th Cir. 1992)... 24
CONTRELL PLUMMER, Plaintiff-Appellant, v. WEXFORD HEALTH SOURCES, INCORPORATED, et al., Defendants-Appellees.No. 14-3314UNITED STATES COURT OF APPEALS FOR THE SEVENTH CIRCUIT 14, 45
David A. Higdon, Plaintiff, vs. Charles L. Ryan, Defendant. No. CV 13-0475-PHX-DGC (JFM).............................. 5
David Arenberg, Plaintiff, vs. Charles Ryan, et al., Defendants.No. CV 10-2228-PHX-MHM (MHB)UNITED STATES DISTRICT COURT FOR THE DISTRICT OF ARIZONA 6
David Standley, Plaintiff, v. Charles Ryan, et al., DefendantsNo. CV 10-1867-PHX-DGC (ECV)UNITED STATES DISTRICT COURT FOR THE DISTRICT OF ARIZONA 10
DAVID WILSON, PLAINTIFF VS. DON NELSON, CORIZON LLC, JAMES PRATT, JOHN HAROLD AND JIM McLEAN,

DEFENDANTS CASE NO. 6:13-CV-6036 UNITED STATES DISTRICT COURT FOR THE WESTERN DISTRICT OF ARKANSAS, HOT SPRINGS DIVISION 31

DAVON LYMON, Plaintiff-Appellant, v. ARAMARK CORPORATION; JOSEPH NEUBAUER; CHARLIE CARRIZALES, Defendants, and WEXFORD CORPORATION, JOHN SANCHEZ; ABNER HERNANDEZ; JOE WILLIAMS; NEW MEXICO DEPARTMENT OF CORRECTIONS, Defendants-Appellees. No. 11-2210 UNITED STATES COURT OF APPEALS FOR THE TENTH CIRCUIT 17, 48

DENNIS JAY WARREN, Plaintiff, v. CORIZON HEALTH, et al., Defendants 3:15-cv-00161-JO 37

DEREK JOHNSON, personal representative of KELLY CONRAD GREEN II, deceased; KELLY CONRAD GREEN and SANDY PULVER, Plaintiffs, v. CORIZON HEALTH, INC., a Tennessee Corporation; LANE COUNTY, an Oregon county; DR. CARL KELDIE, an individual; DR. JUSTIN MONTOYA, an individual; VICKI THOMAS, an individual; KIRSTIN WHITE, an individual;; SHARON EPPERSON (nee FAGAN), an individual, and JACOB PLEICH, an individual, Defendants. 6:13-cv-1855-TC UNITED STATES DISTRICT COURT FOR THE DISTRICT OF OREGON.....30

DiSabatino v US Fidelity & Guaranty Co, 635 F.Supp. 35, 355 (D.De. 1986) 1

DORCUS WITHERS, Plaintiff-Appellant, v. WEXFORD HEALTH SOURCES, INC., et al., Defendants-Appellees.No. 10-3012 UNITED STATES COURT OF APPEALS FOR THE SEVENTH CIRCUIT...16, 46

DURWIN C. BOYD (AIS # 189145), Plaintiff, v. CORIZON INC., Defendant. Civil Action No. 2:13CV354-WHA UNITED STATES DISTRICT COURT FOR THE MIDDLE DISTRICT OF ALABAMA, NORTHERN DIVISION 34

EARL FARMER, Plaintiff, v. C.L. "BUTCH" OTTER; RANDY BLADES; MS. WAMBLE-FISHER; CATHY STEFFEN; CORIZON MEDICAL SERVICES; IDAHO STATE DEPARTMENT OF CORRECTION; and IDAHO STATE BOARD OF CORRECTION, Defendants. Case No. 1:14-cv-00345-BLW UNITED STATES DISTRICT COURT FOR THE DISTRICT OF IDAHO 37

EDUARDO OLMEDO, Plaintiff, -against- CORIZON P.C., DR. JEAN RICHARD, and DR. PARK, Defendants. 14 Civ. 3853 (AT)(HBP) UNITED STATES DISTRICT COURT FOR THE SOUTHERN DISTRICT OF NEW YORK 33

EDWARD E. STEWART, III, Plaintiff, v. MICHAEL WENEROWICZ, DENNIS BRUMFIELD, MICHAEL DOYLE, JOHN HOFER, KEITH VANCLIFF, ROBERT GRUBER, CORIZON HEALTH, INC., RICHARD STEFANIK, M.D., MICHAEL HERBIK, D.O., RAYMOND MARCHAK, P.A., and SUSAN BERRIER, R.N., Defendants. CIVIL ACTION NO. 12-4046 UNITED STATES DISTRICT COURT FOR THE EASTERN DISTRICT OF PENNSYLVANIA 38

EDWIN WYLIE-BIGGS, Plaintiff, vs. ORLANDO L. HARPER; WILLIAM EMERICK; JESSE ANDRASCIK; SIMON WAINWRIGHT; LONG Deputy Warden; CORIZON HEALTH SERVICES, Defendants. Civil Action No. 14-1150 UNITED STATES DISTRICT COURT FOR THE WESTERN DISTRICT OF PENNSYLVANIA 40

Eric SANCHEZ, Plaintiff-Appellant,v.Duane R. VILD, et al., Defendants-Appellees.No. 88-2458.United States Court of Appeals,
Ninth Circuit. 3

Erik Scott Maloney, Plaintiff, vs. Charles L. Ryan, et al., Defendants.No. CV 13-00314-PHX-RCB(BSB) UNITED STATES DISTRICT COURT FOR THE DISTRICT OF ARIZONA 4

FRANCISCO ROBINSON, Plaintiff/Appellant, v. CHARLES RYAN, as Director, Arizona Department of Corrections; Regina Dorsey; Anna Gonzales; David Summers; Karyn Klausner, Defendants/Appellees. No. 1 CA- CV 12-0535COURT OF APPEALS OF ARIZONA, DIVISION ONE 8

Gagan v American cablevision, Inc., 77 F.3d 951, 962-963 (7th Cir. 1996 23

Galen Lloyd Houser, Plaintiff -vs- Charles L. Ryan, et al., Defendants. CV-13-0200-PHX-GMS (JFM)................12, 42

Galen Lloyd Houser, Plaintiff -vs- Charles L. Ryan, et al., Defendants.CV-13-0200-PHX-GMS (JFM)UNITED STATES DISTRICT COURT FOR THE DISTRICT OF ARIZONA 21, 51

HAROLD DAVEY CASSELL ADC # 073885, PLAINTIFF v. CORRECT CARE SOLUTIONS, LLC and CORIZON, INC., DEFENDANTS 5:14CV00403-DPM-JJV UNITED STATES DISTRICT COURT FOR THE EASTERN DISTRICT OF ARKANSAS, PINE BLUFF DIVISION 37, 38

HOYT RAY, Plaintiff-Appellant, v. WEXFORD HEALTH SOURCES, INC., and VIPIN K. SHAH, Defendants-Appellees.No. 12-1774 UNITED STATES COURT OF APPEALS FOR THE SEVENTH CIRCUIT 16, 47

In re Integration Of Nebraska State Bar Assn 275 N.W. 265, 268 (1937) 1

IVES T. ARTIS, Plaintiff, vs. BYUNGHAK JIN, Medical Director (indiviaul Compasity); CORIZON HEALTH, Formerly Prison Healthcare Services (Official Compasity), Defendants. Civil Action No. 13-1226 UNITED STATES DISTRICT COURT FOR THE WESTERN DISTRICT OF PENNSYLVANIA 28

JAMES A. DULAK, Plaintiff, v. CORIZON INC., Dr. HUTCHINSON, Dr. STIEVE, Dr. ABDELLATIF, PA JINDAHL, ROGERS,

TAMMY ROTHHAAR, Defendants. Case No. 14-10193 UNITED STATES DISTRICT COURT FOR THE EASTERN DISTRICT OF MICHIGAN, SOUTHERN DIVISION 32

JAMES COLEN #604910, Plaintiff, v. CORIZON MEDICAL SERVICES, et al., Defendants.Civil Action No.: 14-12948 27

JANET MOSELY, et al., Plaintiffs, v. STATE OF MISSOURI; CORIZON, INC.; IAN WALLACE; TRAVIS WILHITE; and DONNA SPAVEN, Defendants Case No. 1:15CV00052 AGF UNITED STATES DISTRICT COURT FOR THE EASTERN DISTRICT OF MISSOURI, SOUTHEASTERN DIVISION 29

Jeffrey James Faulkner, Plaintiff, vs. Charles Ryan, Defendant.No. CV 10-2441-PHX-SMM (JFM) UNITED STATES DISTRICT COURT FOR THE DISTRICT OF ARIZONA 7

JENNIFER JONES, Plaintiff, v. CORIZON, LLC, et al., Defendants. Case No. 4:15 CV 346 RWSUNITED STATES DISTRICT COURT FOR THE EASTERN DISTRICT OF MISSOURI, EASTERN DIVISION 36

JESSICA HANKEY, Individually, and as Administratrix of the Estate of Ryan Rohrbaugh, Appellant v. WEXFORD HEALTH SOURCES, INC.; PRISON HEALTH SERVICES, INC.; D.O. MARK BAKER; D.O. ALAN ESPER; DEBORAH O'LEARY, PA-C No. 09-3675 UNITED STATES COURT OF APPEALS FOR THE THIRD CIRCUIT 13, 44

JOHN ASHLEY HALE, Plaintiff--Appellant, v. RONALD KING, Superintendent of Southern Mississippi Correctional Institution; MARGARET BINGHAM, Superintendent of Southern Mississippi Correctional Institution; CHRISTOPHER EPPS, Commissioner of Mississippi Department of Corrections; MIKE HATTEN, Health Service Administrator of Wexford for Southern Mississippi Correctional Institution; JOHN DOE, Physician at Southern Mississippi Correctional Institution; DOCTOR ZANDU, Psychiatrist at Central Mississippi Correctional Facility; DOCTOR PATRICK ARNOLD, Physician for Correctional Medical Services at Southern Mississippi Correctional Institution; DOCTOR WILLIAMS, Psychiatrist of Correctional Medical Services for Southern Mississippi Correctional Institution; DOCTOR TRINCA, Physician for Wexford at Southern Mississippi Correctional Institution; MIRIAM MOULDS, Kitchen Supervisor at Southern Mississippi Correctional Institution; JOHN DOE 2, Chief Executive Officer of Correctional Medical Services for Mississippi Department of Corrections; JOHN DOE 3, Chief Executive Officer of Wexford at Southern Mississippi Correctional Institution for Mississippi Department of Corrections; DOCTOR MCCLEAVE; DOCTOR WOODALL; WEXFORD HEALTH SERVICES, Defendants--Appellees. No. 07-60997 UNITED STATES COURT OF APPEALS FOR THE FIFTH CIRCUIT 18, 49

JOHN F. WARREN, Plaintiff, v. CORIZON HEALTH; DR. APRIL DAWSON, M.D.; MICHAEL TAKAGI, PA-C; DIANE DICE, PA-C; STEVEN STEDTFELD, PA-C; DAVID FOSS, NP RYAN VALLEY, HASA; BRISTY DELAOE; JOHN DOE PROVIDER; JANE DOE PROVIDER; STEVEN LITTLE, WARDEN; BRENT REINKE, DIRECTOR OF IDAHO DEPT. OF CORRECTIONS; Defendants. Case No. 1:14-CV-00011-EJLUNITED STATES DISTRICT COURT FOR THE DISTRICT OF IDAHO 35

JOHNNY L. McGOWAN, JR., Plaintiff, v. CORIZON MEDICAL, LT. KEVIN GUNN, DR. CLEMENT BARNARD, and DARREL THOMAS, Defendants.No. 3:14-cv-0578UNITED STATES DISTRICT COURT FOR THE MIDDLE DISTRICT OF TENNESSEE, NASHVILLE DIVISION 36

Joseph Gerald Lee Eldridge, Plaintiff, vs. Charles L. Ryan, et al., Defendants.No. CV 13-0888-PHX-DGC (JFM)UNITED STATES DISTRICT COURT FOR THE DISTRICT OF ARIZONA 7

JUSTIN JAMES HINZO, Plaintiff - Appellant, v. NEW MEXICO CORRECTIONS DEPARTMENT; JOE WILLIAMS; GEORGE TAPIA; WEXFORD HEALTH SOURCES, INC.; CORRECTIONAL MEDICAL SERVICES, INC.; DR. FNU ARNOLD; DR. WILLIAM MIZELL; DR. TONY LNU; DR. DEBRA CLYDE; DR. JOHN STOVER; DR. JOHN DOE (L.C.C.F.); DR. JOHN DOE (C.N.M.C.F.); DR. JOHN DOE (W.N.M.C.F.); DAVID GONZALES, Correctional Officer; WAYNE GALLEGOS; LIANE LOPEZ, R.N.; JERRY ROARK (Deputy Warden); LAWRENCE JARAMILLO, Warden P.N.M.; G.E.O., Defendants - Appellees. 15, 45

Karen Marie Hansen, Plaintiff, vs. Charles Ryan, et al., Defendants. No. CV 09-1290-PHX-GMS (ECV) UNITED STATES DISTRICT COURT FOR THE DISTRICT OF ARIZONA.. 6

KENNETH F. LEONARD, Plaintiff/Appellant, v. FLORIDA DEPARTMENT OF CORRECTIONS, WEXFORD HEALTH SOURCES, INC., DAVID HARRIS, G. SOMODEVILLA, A. PIPIN, J.L. GREEN, AND G.J. SMITH, Defendants/Appellees. 06-11223-FF UNITED STATES COURT OF APPEALS FOR THE ELEVENTH CIRCUIT 14, 44

KENNETH R. HARRISON, #160623, Plaintiff, v. CORIZON MEDICAL SERVICES, Defendant.CIVIL ACTION NO. 2:14-CV-1251-MHTUNITED STATES DISTRICT COURT FOR THE MIDDLE DISTRICT OF ALABAMA, EASTERN DIVISION.. 29

Kevin Mitchell, Plaintiff, v. Corizon Health, Inc., et al., Defendants. No. CV 14-1754-PHX-DGC (BSB)UNITED STATES DISTRICT COURT FOR THE DISTRICT OF ARIZONA.. 26

LEONARD T. WILLIAMSON, Appellant v. WEXFORD HEALTH SOURCES, INC.; STATE CORRECTIONAL INSTITUTION, at Pittsburgh (SCIP) Medical Department; DON GEORGE, RN; BONNIE BELL, RN; RACHELLE, RN; NOEL RANKIN, RN; MARSHA HANCOCK, RN; TOM MCDONOUGH, PHYSICIANS ASSISTANT NO. 04-3481 UNITED STATES COURT OF APPEALS FOR THE THIRD CIRCUIT 21, 51

Living Designs Inc., et al., v   E.I.DuPont De Nemours And Company, et. Al., 431 F.3d 353 (9th Cir. 2005) 1, 23

MANNIE MADDOX, Plaintiff--Appellant, v. WEXFORD HEALTH SOURCES, INC., et al., Defendnts--Appellees.No. 12-1810UNITED STATES COURT OF APPEALS FOR THE SEVENTH CIRCUIT 15, 46

Mark E. Hampton, Plaintiff, vs. Charles Ryan, et al., Defendants.No. CV 03-1706-PHX-NVW 8

MARK FRENCH, Plaintiff, v CORIZON, et al., Defendants Civil Action No. JFM-14-2263 UNITED STATES DISTRICT COURT FOR THE DISTRICT OF MARYLAND 28

MAURICE D. HARPER, Plaintiff, v. CORIZON, LOUIS GIORLA, MICHELLE FARRELL, FRANK ABELLO, MARIEL TRIMBLE, and PANTAL JEAN, Defendants. CIVIL ACTION No. 14-639 30

MAURICE D. HARPER, Plaintiff, v. CORIZON, LOUIS GIORLA, MICHELLE FARRELL, FRANK ABELLO, MARIEL TRIMBLE, and PANTAL JEAN, Defendants. CIVIL ACTION No. 14-639 UNITED STATES DISTRICT COURT FOR THE EASTERN DISTRICT OF PENNSYLVANIA 30

MCM Partners Inc v Andrews-Bartlett & Assoc. Inc, 62 F.3d 967 (7th Cir. 1995) 24

Miranda v Ponce Fed. Bank, 948 F.2d 41, 44 (1st Cir. 1991) 22

Mylan Lab Inc v Matkari, 7 F.3d 1130 (4th Cir.1993) 24

OSMONDO SMITH, Plaintiff, -against- CORIZON HEALTH SERVICES and THE CITY OF NEW YORK, Defendants. 14 Civ. 08839 (GBD)(SN) UNITED STATES DISTRICT COURT FOR THE SOUTHERN DISTRICT OF NEW YORK 35

OSVALDO C. PALAZON, RONNIE E. CONNOLLY, COLLINS MURRAY, RICARDO PEREZ, WILLIAM BISHOP, WILLIE JONES, AARON KOSBERG, DANIEL MAGLIO, AUSTIN SPEAS, Plaintiffs, KENNETH MCKENNA, Plaintiff-Appellant, versus SECRETARY FOR THE DEPARTMENT OF CORRECTIONS, WEXFORD HEALTH SOURCES INC., DR. HARIDAS NARSI BHADJA, DENISE KELCHNER, Defendants-Appellees, FLORIDA CORRECTIONAL MEDICAL AUTHORITY, Defendant. No. 07-14451 UNITED STATES COURT OF APPEALS FOR THE ELEVENTH CIRCUIT 19, 49

PAUL GRAHAME MORGAN, Plaintiff-Appellant v. STATE OF MISSISSIPPI; ATTORNEY GENERAL OF THE STATE OF MISSISSIPPI; CHRISTOPHER EPPS; E.L. SPARKMAN; RONALD KING; LAWRENCE KELLY; MARGARET BINGHAM; BOBBY KING; DR. BEARRY; RUTHIE HALL, Nurse; MILLIS WASHINGTON; DR. ARNOLD; DR. WALKER; LT. HOLMES; DR. WATTS; DR. MCCLEAVE; DR. RON WOODALL; LIEUTENANT "UNKNOWN" BONNER; CAPTAIN UNKNOWN DAVIS;EMIL DANEFF; WEXFORD HEALTH SOURCES, INC.; JOHN DOE, I, CEO of Correctional Medical Services; JOHN DOE, II, CEO of Wexford Health Sources, Inc.; JASON HOLMES; HUBERT DAVIS; RITA BONNER; CAPTAIN PAGE; CAPTAIN ENLERS; CAPTAIN SIMMS; BRENDA SIMMS; NINA ENLERS; SHARON PAIGE, Defendants-Appellees No. 09-60959 UNITED STATES COURT OF APPEALS FOR THE FIFTH CIRCUIT 18, 48

Peter Sotelo, Plaintiff, vs. Terry Stewart; Donna Clement; Charles Ryan; Meg Savage; Dora Shriro, et. al., Defendants.No. CV 03-1668-PHX-NVW UNITED STATES DISTRICT COURT FOR THE DISTRICT OF ARIZONA 9

Redman v County Of San Diego, 942 F.2d 1435, 1445 (9th Cir. 1991)(en banc) 11, 22

Reeves v Ernest Young, 507 U.S. 170 (1993) 23

Riehle v. Margolies, 279 U.S. 218, 225 (1929) 1

Robert F. Lindley, Jr., Plaintiff, vs. Charles L. Ryan, et al., Defendants. No. CV 12-1422-PHX-DGC (MEA) UNITED STATES DISTRICT COURT FOR THE DISTRICT OF ARIZONA 3

Robert Joseph Benge, Plaintiff, v. Charles L. Ryan, et al., Defendants.No. CV 14-0402-PHX-DGC (BSB)UNITED STATES DISTRICT COURT FOR THE DISTRICT OF ARIZONA 12, 43

RODERIC R. McDOWELL, Plaintiff-Appellant, versus PERNELL BROWN, JOHN DOE, No. 1 WEXFORD HEALTH SOURCES, INC., et al., Defendants-Appellees. No. 04-10272 UNITED STATES COURT OF APPEALS FOR THE ELEVENTH CIRCUIT 21, 51

RONALD C. MACON, JR., Plaintiff-Appellant, v. SYLVIA MAHONE, DENNIS LARSON, and WEXFORD HEALTH SOURCES, INC., Defendants-Appellees. No. 13-2155 UNITED STATES COURT OF APPEALS FOR THE SEVENTH CIRCUIT 14, 15, 45

ROOSEVELT THOMAS, JR., AIS #115280, Plaintiff, vs. CORIZON, INC., Defendant. CIVIL ACTION 15-68-WS-M UNITED STATES DISTRICT COURT FOR THE SOUTHERN DISTRICT OF ALABAMA, SOUTHERN DIVISION 38

RUTH DENHAM, as personal representative for the estate of Tracy Lee Veira, Plaintiff, v. CORIZON HEALTH, INC. and VOLUSIA COUNTY, a political subdivision of the State of Florida, Defendants. 35

SALVATORE CHIMENTI, Appellant v. ROGER KIMBER, Medical Director; BADDICK, Regional Director; ROWE,

Wexford Health Sources, Inc.; I. KAUFER, Wexford Health Sources, Inc.; C. POLLOCK, Site Coordinator; FARROHK MOHADJERIN, Former Medical Director; MARTIN F. HORN; ROBERT S. BITNER, Chief Hearing Examiner for the D.O.C.; FREDERICK K. FRANK; PAT YARGER, SCI-Huntingdon Medical Department; P. E. EVERHART, SCI-Huntingdon Medical Department NO. 03-2056 UNITED STATES COURT OF APPEALS FOR THE THIRD CIRCUIT 20, 50

SCOTT RICHARD HANSON, Plaintiffs, v. JOHANNA SMITH, DR. SCOTT DAVID LOSSMAN; DR. APRIL CHARLENE DAWSON; DR. MYUNG AE SONG DO; MS. RONA SIEGERT; JOHN and JANE DOES, One through Ten; CORRECTIONAL MEDICAL SERVICES; and CORIZON MEDICAL SERVICES, Defendants. Case No. 1:11-cv-00525-BLW UNITED STATES DISTRICT COURT FOR THE DISTRICT OF IDAHO 31

Shaka, Plaintiff, v. Charles Ryan, et al., Defendants.No. CV 10-2253-PHX-SMM (BSB) 8

Sheldon Walker, Plaintiff, v. Charles L. Ryan, et al., Defendants.No. CV-14-02554-PHX-DJH ZB) UNITED STATES DISTRICT COURT FOR THE DISTRICT OF ARIZONA 10

SOTINA LAVALE CUFFEE, deceased, Estate of, by and through her administrator, Bradley A. Cuffee, Plaintiff - Appellant, v. JOHN R. NEWHART, individually and in his official capacity as Sheriff of the City of Chesapeake, Defendant - Appellee, v. WEXFORD HEALTH SOURCES, INCORPORATED, Third Party Defendant - Appellee.No. 10-1494UNITED STATES COURT OF APPEALS FOR THE FOURTH CIRCUIT 17, 47

STEVE ODOM, Plaintiff, v. CORIZON, INC., et al, Defendants. Case No. 1:14-CV-606 36

TERRY DAVIS, Plaintiff, v. CORIZON, et al., Defendants. Case No. 5:13-cv-0949-CLS-TMP UNITED STATES DISTRICT COURT FOR THE NORTHERN DISTRICT OF ALABAMA, NORTHEASTERN DIVISION 32

Thomas Bartholomew Layden, IV, Plaintiff, v. Charles L. Ryan, Corizon Incorporated, Michael Hegmann, Subodh Shroff, Alison Scott, Matthew Musson, Richard Pratt, Kamal Rastogi, Defendants. No. CV 14-02470 PHX DJH (DMF) UNITED STATES DISTRICT COURT FOR THE DISTRICT OF ARIZONA 27

THOMAS EDWARD JONES, #140289, Plaintiff, v. CORIZON, et al., Defendants.CASE NO. 2:12-CV-786-WHA [WO]UNITED STATES DISTRICT COURT FOR THE MIDDLE DISTRICT OF ALABAMA, NORTHERN DIVISION 32

Thomas M. James, Plaintiff, vs. Charles L. Ryan, et al., Defendants. No. CV 10-0510-PHX-GMS (JFM) UNITED STATES DISTRICT COURT FOR THE DISTRICT OF ARIZONA 5

Thomas Stewart, Jr., Plaintiff, vs. Charles L. Ryan, et al., Defendants.No. CV 12-0719-PHX-RCB (LOA)UNITED STATES DISTRICT COURT FOR THE DISTRICT OF ARIZONA 10

TIMOTHY G PRYER, Plaintiff-Appellant v. R. WALKER, Doctor/Health Services Administrator at CMCF III; SHARON PAIGE, Captain, Central MS Correctional Facility III; DR. JOSEPH BLACKSTON; CORRECTIONAL HEALTH SERVICE, INC.; WEXFORD HEALTHCARE RESOURCES; COMMISSIONER CHRISOPHER EPPS; MARGARET BINGHAM, Defendants-AppelleesNo. 08-60867   UNITED STATES COURT OF APPEALS FOR THE FIFTH CIRCUIT 13, 43

TOMMY WHITE, SR., Plaintiff-Appellant v. CHRISTOPHER B. EPPS, COMMISSIONER, MISSISSIPPI DEPARTMENT OF CORRECTIONS; RON KING, Superintendent, South Mississippi Correctional Institution-Two; DR. RON WOODALL; NURSE HAM; WEXFORD HEALTH; NURSE APRIL MEGS, Defendants-AppelleesNo. 10-60556 UNITED STATES COURT OF APPEALS FOR THE FIFTH CIRCUIT 12, 43

United States v Qunitanilla, 2 F.3d 1469, 1485 (7th Cir. 1993) 24

VICTOR ANTONIO PARSONS; SHAWN JENSEN; STEVE SWARTZ; DUSTIN BRISLAN; SONIA RODRIGUEZ; CHRISTINA VERDUZCO; JACKIE THOMAS; JEREMY SMITH; ROBERT CARRASCO GAMEZ, JR.; MARYANNE CHISHOLM; DESIREE LICCI; JOSEPH HEFNER; JOSHUA POLSON; CHARLOTTE WELLS; ARIZONA CENTER FOR DISABILITY LAW, Plaintiffs-Appellees, v. CHARLES L. RYAN; RICHARD PRATT, Defendants-Appellants. No. 13-16396 UNITED STATES COURT OF APPEALS FOR THE NINTH CIRCUIT 3

WILLIAM L. LANE, Plaintiff-Appellant, v. WEXFORD HEALTH SOURCES (CONTREATOR); VANESSA SAWYER, Health Care Administrator; PAMILA REDDEN, Defendants-Appellees. 16, 47

William Mark Isbell, Plaintiff, vs. Charles Ryan, et al., Defendants. No. CV 11-0391-PHX-JAT (JFM) UNITED STATES DISTRICT COURT FOR THE DISTRICT OF ARIZONA 5

WILLIAM R. TUBBS, PLAINTIFF ADC # 120585, v. CORIZON, INC.; et al., DEFENDANTS 5:13CV00377-BSM-JJV UNITED STATES DISTRICT COURT FOR THE EASTERN DISTRICT OF ARKANSAS, PINE BLUFF DIVISION 29

Statutes

18 U.S.C. 1961 etc. seq 22

18 U.S.C. 1961(3) 23

REMEDY AND REDEMPTION

18 U.S.C. 1961(4) 23, 25
18 U.S.C. 1965(a). 23, 25, 41
Title 28 U.S.C. 1331(1 2

Rules
Federal Rules Of Civil Procedure 26 through 37 22
of Federal Rules Of Civil Procedure 26 through 37 11

Treatises
Wright Miler & Kane, Fed.   Prac. & Proc. Civil 2d. at 870, Page 412. 1